MANUAL FOR TRANSFERS OF RIGHTS OF OCCUPANCY

MANUAL FOR TRANSFERS OF RIGHTS OF OCCUPANCY

Zebron Steven Gondwe

MKUKI NA NYOTA PUBLISHERS
P.O.Box 4246, Dar Es Salaam Tanzania.

Mkuki na Nyota Publishers
6 Muhonda, Mission Quarter Kariakoo
P. O. Box 4246, Dar es Salaam, Tanzania

ISBN 9976-973-88 8

For Doris

Who has a claim against me that I must pay?
Everything under heaven belongs to me.
Job 41: 11

Table of Contents

Table of Contents

Foreword

It is not very often that an academic dares to prepare a manual for practitioners. Dr. Gondwe has taken this rare step. Fortunately, he is amply qualified to do so. He has taught land law at the University of Dar es Salaam for many years. He has also practised law, particularly conveyancing, with a practising firm for a considerable number of years. This gives Dr. Gondwe an enviable edge and he has made good use of it in this manual.

As will become apparent to a perceptive user of the manual, the state of law, so far as land transfers are concerned, is not in the best of shape. The hesitancy of the author in taking definite positions is therefore understandable. Controversies surround a number of aspects of land transfers. Take, for example, the issue of the Commissioner's consent without which the contract is said to be inoperative. The full bench of the Court of Appeal set out to put this controversy to rest in the case *Abualy Alibhai Azizi v. Bhatia Brothers Ltd* (1999) (discussed in Chapter 3 of the manual). I share the author's view though that not all the issues surrounding lack of consent were adequately addressed by the Court. The full implication of the *Abualy* decision, however, will have to await further case law.

Dr. Gondwe has also made a bold attempt to make references to the relevant portions of the new Land Act, 1999 and the Village Land Act, 1999. For reasons, which should be obvious, the author's treatment of the new laws can only be perfunctory at this stage. We have yet to see how these Acts will work in practice when they are finally brought into force. I have no doubt though that Dr. Gondwe will be able to give us a more critical appreciation of the new laws in the second edition of the manual.

Let me end by expressing my appreciation of this venture. Academics in countries like ours have to double up in writing not only usual academic textbooks but also even manuals for practitioners. This is so because our practitioners have neither the time nor the inclination to indulge in any writing, let alone that of well considered manuals. In this regard, I hope, Dr. Gondwe's example will be followed by other similarly placed academics. We owe it to the younger generation of practitioners who feel a great need for such books to guide them through the labyrinth of mostly contradictory, and worse, unreported case law.

Issa G, Shivji
Professor of Law,
Advocate of the High Court of
Tanzania & Zanzibar,
Chairman of the Presidential Commission
Of Inquiry into Land Matters and
Executive Director of the Land Rights Research
and Resources Institute (HAKIARDHI).

Dar es Salaam,
November 1999

Acknowledgement

This work would not have become a reality without the support of certain individuals and institutions. In that respect, the author is indebted to Mr. Nimrod E. Mkono of Mkono & Company, Advocates for invaluable schooling in law practice and for being the initial inspiration for this work, the late Mrs. Clotilda Mlenge for word processing the first draft of the manuscript and Ms. Rukia Mwaba for word processing the second draft of the manuscript. I am indebted to Prof. G. M. Fimbo and Dr. W.B.L. Kapinga for their helpful hints and wise counsel during the preparation of the manuscript. I must also thank Mr. Senen Edmund Mponda of Mkono & Company for supplying me with a complement of very useful cases.

I am profoundly indebted to several individuals for reading the manuscript and making very useful observations and suggestions. They are Dr. Ringo W. Tenga of the Faculty of Law, University of Dar es Salaam and also of the law firm of Law Associates; Prof. Chris Maina Peter of the Faculty of Law, University of Dar es Salaam; Mr. Ngassa Mbassa Dindi, Senior Legal Council in the Presidential Parastatal Sector Reform Commission, also of Mkono & Company and formerly a Lecturer in law at the Institute of Finance Management; and, Mr. Fidelis K. Mutakyamirwa, Principal Assistant Registrar of Titles and Officer-in-Charge of the Legal Section in the Land Services Division of the Ministry of Lands and Human Settlement Development I am especially indebted to Mr. Mutakyamirwa for his exemplary commitment and interest in the project.

Very special thanks go to The Honourable Mr. Justice Lameck M. Mfalila, Justice of Appeal of the Court of Appeal of Tanzania and Prof. Issa G. Shivji of the Faculty of Law, University of Dar es Salaam and also the Executive Director of the Land Rights Research and Resources Institute, better known as "HakiArdhi". These two eminent persons were able to find time in their very busy schedules to read the manuscript and grace it with their vast experience in land matters.

I thank the University of Dar es Salaam for its ever present and consistent support to my academic and professional development. Much has been achieved over the years from that support.

Finally, I thank my son, Stephen Kamanga Gondwe, "Gigi", for sitting by my side, giving me company, throughout the preparation of the manuscript. I derived unique inspiration from his ever present question: "*Baba*, when will you finish this work?"

Introduction

There are many types of disposition of land, but in this work it's the transfer of Right of Occupancy alone, which concerns us. Persons involved, or interested, in transfers of Rights of Occupancy frequently encounter procedural problems. With that in mind, this manual attempts to deal with the main aspects of transfer of Rights of Occupancy. Part One of this work sets down and examines the law governing the transfer of Rights of Occupancy. It also summarizes principles regulating the ownership of land in **Mainland Tanzania** (in some legislation referred to as "Tanzania" and even "Tanganyika") and the acquisition and transfer of Rights of Occupancy.

Part Two is the actual manual for transfer of Rights of Occupancy, comprising of a checklist of the steps constituting a transfer, a matrix showing the circulation of some essential documents and several annexes. The checklist sets out the procedure for transfer of Rights of Occupancy, while the annexes present in some detail the relevant statutory provisions, specimen forms, scales of duties and fees payable. For the sake of clarity, in many places the principles examined in Part One are cross-referenced with the annexes set out in Part Two.

The work where appropriate, has of course employed the wording, terms and definitions found in applicable statutes. But the text is virtually devoid of legal complexity and will hopefully offer invaluable ready-reference guidance. It should prove to be of interest to land administrators, legal practitioners, investors and the general public. It is likely, in addition, to have particular appeal to teachers and students of land law who, alas, tend to have little time to grapple with details of the law and procedure governing the transfer of Rights of Occupancy.

While the manuscript was still under preparation, the National Assembly of the United Republic of Tanzania, on 11 February 1999, enacted the **Land Act**, 1999. The Act obtained Presidential assent on 15 May 1999 whereupon it became law, but **it has not come into operation** because the Minister responsible for lands has not yet appointed the date(s) of commencement. That may be so because the preparation of subsidiary legislation, including prescribed forms, that will guide the operationalisation of the Act has yet to be finalised. Provision under the Act repeals key land legislation like the **Land Ordinance** and the **Land (Law of Property and Conveyancing) Ordinance.** The desirability of a preview of such of its provisions as are relevant to this work cannot, therefore, be overemphasized. **Although the preview is in present tense, the reader is minded that at the time of writing the Act was not yet in force.**

PART ONE

PRINCIPLES GOVERNING THE ACQUISITION AND TRANSFER OF RIGHT OF OCCUPANCY

CHAPTER ONE

OWNERSHIP OF LAND

1.1 Public Land

1.1.1 Customary tenure was first disrupted under German rule. About 1,300,000 acres (1% of Tanganyika) of choice land was transferred to settlers in "Conveyances of Ownership" under section 6 of the German **Imperial Decree**, 1895[1]. The British administration recognized German titles and, in fact, enacted provision under which they could be converted into conventional freeholds.[2] In 1923, under section 3 of the **Land Ordinance**,[3] save for title to land or any interest therein lawfully acquired before the commencement of the Ordinance, the whole of the lands of Mainland Tanzania (Tanganyika) whether occupied or unoccupied were declared to be "public land".

1.1.2 The statutory basis for the concept "public land" today is still section 3 of the **Land Ordinance**. The declaration covered about 99% of the land. The balance of 1%, held under freehold tenure, was exempted from the declaration.[4] The **Freehold Titles (Conversion) and Government Leases Act**[5] extinguished all freeholds on 1 July 1963, whereupon such tenure became part of public land. Following the extinction of freeholds, the ownership of the whole of the lands of Tanganyika became public and individuals could no longer, in a general sense, **own** land in Tanganyika.

1.1.3 Under section 3 of the **Government Leaseholds (Conversion to Rights of Occupancy) Act**, 1969,[6] all Government Leases were converted to Rights of Occupancy effective 1 April 1970.[7] As of that date, there is only one tenure in this country: the "Right of Occupancy", which is either granted under section 6 of the **Land Ordinance** or is held under native laws and customs but is recognised under section 2 of that Ordinance.[8]

1.1.4 This work deals with the transfer of the Right of Occupancy granted under section 6 of the **Land Ordinance**. Such Right has come to be known as the "Granted Right of Occupancy". But in this work it will simply be referred to as a "Right of Occupancy."

1..2 National Land Policy, 1995

1.2.1 Prof. R.W. James said that, "No study of the land laws of Tanzania that omits a consideration of land policy would be of any value or use to our students."[9] Since Tanzania attained political independence on 9 December 1961, there has been the need to have a comprehensive land policy that would govern land tenure, land use management and administration.[10] The new **National Land Policy**,[11] which was introduced in June 1995, is the result of extensive consultation and deliberation. It incorporates the position of the Government on the **Report of the Presidential Commission of Inquiry into Land Matters**[12] reached by the Cabinet on 22 December 1994, the recommendations and observations of the National Workshop on Land Policy held at Arusha from 16 to 18 January 1995 and comments and suggestions from the public and mass media.[13]

1.2.2 Amongst matters also considered at that Workshop, but which were not, eventually, included in the **National Land Policy** or the **Land Act**, 1999[14] include the reintroduction of freehold tenure;[15] divesting the President of the reversionary[16] (some call it "radical") title;[17] the vesting of "national land" in a "Land Commission";[18] and, vesting of village land in the "Village Assembly."[19] Suffice it to say that divesting the President of the reversionary title would, effectively, have brought "public land", as we now know it, to an end. As regards transfers, it will transpire in the course of this work that virtually all recommendations made by the Presidential Commission of Inquiry Into Land Matters concerning dispositions have either been incorporated into the **Land Act**, 1999 or will feature prominently under other legislation that is now on the drawing table.[20]

1.2.3 The Government is convinced that implementation of the Policy offers the best opportunity to bring about, in a responsible and orderly fashion, a land dispensation which is economically sound and compatible with the aspirations of Tanzania. At the same time it is being ensured, under the Policy, that the tried and tested juridical basis on which existing land rights and existing patterns of community order are regulated will remain intact.[21]

1.2.4 The National Land Policy reiterates and retains the four central land tenure tenets in a modified form as follows:

a) land is owned by the public and is vested in the President as a trustee on behalf of the citizens;

b) speculation on land will be controlled;

c) rights of occupancy whether statutory or customary are and will continue to be the only recognized type of land tenure; and,

d) rights and title to land under any consolidated or new land law will continue to be based mainly on use and occupation.

1.2.5 The overall aim of the **National Land Policy** is to promote and ensure a secure land tenure system, to encourage the optimal use of land resources, and to facilitate broad based social and economic development without upsetting or endangering the ecological balance of the environment.[22] By creating an efficient institutional framework or structure for land administration which is also transparent, the Government hopes that the Policy should help streamline and simplify the procedures for getting land rather than making them cumbersome as they are at present, thus reducing public complaints regarding land administration.[23]

1.2.6 The statutory bases for "public land" under the **Land Act**, 1999[24], are sections 3(1)(a) and 4(1). Under section 3(1)(a) of the Act, for example, it is provided that among the

Fundamental Principles of the **National Land Policy**, which it is the objective of that Act to promote and to which all persons exercising powers under applying or interpreting that Act are to have regard to, is to recognize that all land in Tanzania is public land vested in the President as trustee on behalf of all citizens.[25] But the operational provision is section 4(1) of the Act, which provides that all land in Tanzania **shall continue** to be public land and remain vested in the President as trustee for and on behalf of all the citizens of Tanzania. This latter provision confirms that, as regards the concept "public land", there is no break with the past. Provisions of the **Land Act**, 1999, which are relevant to transfers of Rights of Occupancy are examined in Chapter 2 and Chapter 3 of this manual, in particular in Chapter 3 in the section titled "Other Relevant Provisions Under the **Land Act**, 1999".

---

[1] Its full title was, **The Imperial Decree regarding Creation, Acquisition and Conveyance of Crown Lands and regarding the Acquisition and Conveyance of Lands in general in German East Africa**. It was promulgated on 26 November 1895. Its English translation is in **Extracts From German Ordinances and Decrees of German East Africa** (General Headquarters: East African Force, 1916), pp. 129 to 130. Refer to **German Book**, Vol. 1. Chapter 4, p.212. Said section 6 also provided for the transfer of Crown Land to settlers through Leases. But most settlers preferred the Conveyance of Ownership because of its obvious attraction as compared to the Lease. In fact provision did exist for the upgrading of a Lease into a Conveyance of Ownership in fitting circumstances.

[2] Section 7(1) of the **Land Registry Ordinance**, 1923,Ordinance No. 15 of 1923, Chapter 116 of the Laws, repealed under section 115(1) of the **Land Registration Ordinance**.

[3] Ordinance No. 3 of 1923, Chapter 113 of the Laws. The Ordinance is earmarked for repeal under section 183 of the **Land Act**, 1999.

[4] Proviso to section 3 of the **Land Ordinance**.

[5] Act No. 24 of 1963, Chapter 523 of the Laws. That Act was repealed under section 10 of the **Government Leaseholds (Conversion to Rights of Occupancy) Act**, 1969, Act No. 44 of 1969.

[6] Act No. 44 of 1969.

[7] **The Date of Commencement of the Government Leaseholds (Conversion to Rights of Occupancy) Act, 1969 Regulations**, Government Notice No. 85 of 1970, made under section 1(2) of the Act.

[8] The evolution of tenure from the turn of the eighteenth century has enjoyed extensive coverage in various places. See, for example, R.W. James, **Land Tenure**

and Policy in Tanzania (Dar es Salaam: East African Literature Bureau, 1971) pp. 11 to 31 and Chapters 4 and 5; Andrew Bremmer Lyall, **Land Law and Policy in Tanganyika 1919-1932**, LL. M , Dissertation, University of Dar es Salaam, 1973 (unpublished) pp. Chapter 3; R. W. James and G. M. Fimbo, Customary Land Law of Tanzania – A Source Book (Dar es Salaam: East African Literature Bureau, 1973) Chapter 11; and, G. M. Fimbo, "Land, Socialism and the Law in Tanzania" in **Towards Ujamaa – Twenty Years of TANU Leadership**, ed., Gabriel Ruhumbika (Dar es Salaam: East African Literature Bureau, 1974) pp. 232 to 246.

[9] James, **Land Tenure and Policy in Tanzania**, op. cit., p. vii.

[10] **National Land Policy**, The Ministry of Lands, Housing and Urban Development, Dar es Salaam, Tanzania, June 1995, p. 1.

[11] **National Land Policy**, The Ministry of Lands, Housing and Urban Development, Dar es Salaam, Tanzania, June 1995. .

[12] United Republic of Tanzania, **Report of the Presidential Commission of Inquiry Into Land Matters**, Volume 1Land Policy and Land Tenure Structure, November 1992. The need for a new land policy was extensively discussed in Chapter 14, at pp. 140 to 150 of the Report.

[13] **National Land Policy**, op. cit., p. ii.

[14] Act No. 4 of 1999.

[15] This, however, was not a recommendation of the Presidential Commission of Inquiry Into Land Matters.

[16] According to P.G. Osborn, **A Concise Law Dictionary for Students and Practitioners**, Fifth Edition (London: Sweet and Maxwell, 1964), at p. 282, where land is granted by the owner for a less estate or interest than he himself has, his undisposed of interest is termed the "reversion", because the land will revert to the owner on the determination of the particular estate. The estate created by the grant is called the particular estate, and tenure exists between the reversioner (the owner of the reversion) and the tenant.

[17] The vesting of "national land" in "National Lands Commission", and village lands in Village Assemblies, as recommended by the Presidential Commission of Inquiry Into Land Matters, would have given rise to precisely this result. See also footnote 12, *infra*. Conceptually, "reversionary" title and "radical" title are, substantially, the same. See, for example, **Report of the Presidential Commission of Inquiry Into Land Matters**, op. cit., p.152, para. 7 and, especially, para. 8.

[18] See, **Report of the Presidential Commission of Inquiry Into Land Matters**, op. cit., p.151, para 3.

[19] *Ibid*., para 4.

[20] It must be said that, contrary to popular belief, the **National Land Policy** and the **Land Act**, 1999, save for such departures as are set out in para 1.3 above, have by large measure taken in the recommendations of the Presidential Commission of Inquiry Into Land Matters.

[21] **National Land Policy**, op. cit., p. ii.

[22] **National Land Policy**, op. cit., p.5.

[23] **National Land Policy**, op. cit., p. 42.

[24] Act No. 4 of 1999. The Bill came out in, The United Republic of Tanzania, ***BILL SUPPLEMENT*** No. 5, 25 September 1998 to the Gazette of the United Republic of Tanzania No. 39 Vol. 79 dated 25 September 1998.

[25] See page 3 and paragraph 4.1.1 (i) at page 9 of the **National Land Policy**.

CHAPTER TWO

ACQUISTION OF PUBLIC LAND BY INDIVIDUALS AND INSTITUTIONS

2.1 Control and Disposition of Public Land

2.1.1 The control and disposition of public land is, under section 4 of the **Land Ordinance**, vested in the President. The President's status in that behalf somehow resembles that of a trustee in a trust;[26] the property which is the subject matter of such "trust" is public land and citizens of Tanganyika at large are the beneficial owners.[27] But the resemblance stops there because "public land" connotes an **administrative**, rather than a **legal**, relation between the President and public land.[28] Indeed, the vesting provision, that is to say section 4 of the **Land Ordinance**, does not even mention the word "trust" or "trustee".

2.1.2 The concepts "trust" and "beneficial owner(s)" have to be seen in the light of Policy Statements[29] made under the **National Land Policy**. The **National Land Policy** covers various land-related aspects, but its principal goal appears to be "a clearly defined institutional hierarchy for land administration."[30] The Policy states that, land is a constitutional category;[31] land has value;[32] the rights and interests of citizens in land shall not be taken without due process of law; full and fair compensation shall be paid when land is acquired;[33] and, the power of the Executive with respect to land administration will be subject to limitations embedded in law and procedure.

2.1.3 The **Land Act**, 1999, under sections 3(1)(a) and 4(1), has retained substantially the same arrangement. But, unlike section 4 of the **Land Ordinance**, section 4 of the **Land Act**, 1999 expressly vests public land in the President as trustee for and on behalf of all citizens of Tanzania. It remains to be seen whether it will be possible for the

President to sue, or for a citizen of Tanzania to sue the President, in his capacity as a "trustee". Indeed, the structure of the **National Land Policy** and even the **Land Act**, 1999, suggests that the draftsman did not wish to establish a legal relation between the President and public land, and that he had in mind merely an administrative relation in the sense that such land has been placed in its entirety under Government control.

2.1.4 In so far as the objective of that Act is to promote the **National Land Policy**,[34] the "control and disposition" over public land previously enjoyed by the President under the **Land Ordinance** has been scaled down. For example, under section 3(1)(h) and (i) of the **Land Act**, 1999, Fundamental Principles of the **National Land Policy** include the provision of an efficient, effective, economical and **transparent** system of land administration.[35] Also that such system should enable all citizens to participate in making decisions in matters connected with their occupation or use of land.[36] Such principles negate the vesting of the control and disposition of all public land in a single person, namely, the President.[37] The rationale therefor is that the President cannot, alone, perform the administrative and managerial activities envisaged under the **National Land Policy**.

2.1.5 In result, policy matters will be passed on to the Minister while day to day administrative and managerial duties shall be performed by appropriate officials and, or, authorities.[38] Indeed, this is has been the practice in the Ministry of Lands, even though the **Land Ordinance** is not as comprehensive as the **Land Act**, 1999.

2.1.6 To varying degrees, control and disposition of public land is now vested in the Minister responsible for lands,[39] the Commissioner for Lands[40] and Land Allocation Committees.[41] Local Government Authorities have been relegated to a largely advisory role.[42]

2.2 The Right of Occupancy and its Incidents

2.2.1 An individual can occupy and use public land by way of a Right of Occupancy. The term "Right of Occupancy" is defined under section 2 of the **Land Ordinance** as the title to the use and occupation of land and includes the title of a native[43] or native community lawfully using or occupying land in accordance with native law and custom.[44] The holder of a Right of Occupancy is called an occupier,[45] a term that underscores the usufruct[46] character of the Right as opposed to outright ownership. The definition gives rise to two types of Rights of Occupancy: the **granted** Right of Occupancy and the **deemed** Right of Occupancy.[47] The latter, also known as **customary** Right of Occupancy, is outside the purview of this manual because customary law and practice governs it.[48] Nevertheless, it is possible to transform a **customary** Right of Occupancy into a **granted** Right of Occupancy by having the material land surveyed and obtaining and registering a Certificate of Occupancy therefor, whereupon this manual will apply to the resultant granted Right of Occupancy.

2.2.2 Even under the **Land Act**, 1999, the rights that a "rights holder" will be able to enjoy include the granted Right of Occupancy and the customary Right of Occupancy.[49] Except for dropping references to "native"[50] and "native community", the **Land Act**, 1999 substantially re-enacts the current definition of Right of Occupancy. Under section 2 of that Act, "Right of Occupancy" means a title to the use and occupation of land including the title of a **Tanzanian citizen of African descent** or a **community of Tanzanian citizens of African descent** using or occupying land in accordance with customary law.[51] The whole of Part Vl of the **Land Act**, 1999 is devoted to the nature, extent and incidents of granted Rights of Occupancy, which in this work shall simply be referred to as "Right(s) of Occupancy".

2.2.3 Under section 6 of the **Land Ordinance**, 1923, the President may, where it appears to him to be in the general interests of Tanganyika (Mainland Tanzania), grant Right(s) of Occupancy over public land for a maximum term of 99 years. Grants for less than 5 years are called "Short Term Rights of Occupancy" while grants exceeding 5 years are called "Long Term Rights of Occupancy".[52] In practice, grants of Short Term Rights of Occupancy are rarely made.[53] They are normally granted over land in respect of which there is no planning scheme under the provisions of the **Town and Country Planning Ordinance**.[54] But the growth of the informal sector in recent years may revive interest in such Rights of Occupancy.[55] It is no accident, therefore, that even the **Land Act**, 1999 provides that a Right of Occupancy may be granted from year to year of for periods of less than a year determinable by the Commissioner by one year's notice or less, whether or not the grant includes an initial fixed term, so long as that initial fixed term does not exceed 4 years.[56] But, unlike the **Land Ordinance**,[57] the **Land Act**, 1999 does not provide for the grant of a Right of Occupancy at will.

2.2.3 Under section 10 (1) of the **Land Ordinance**, it shall not be lawful for the President to revoke a Right of Occupancy save for "good cause".[58] Good cause includes breach of any term or condition contained or to be implied in the Certificate of Occupancy,[59] or breach of any regulations under that Ordinance relating to the transfer of or dealings with Rights of Occupancy or interests therein.[60] Section 10 (2) of the **Land Ordinance** empowers the President to revoke a Right of Occupancy in the "public interest".[61] Public interest is not defined under that Ordinance, and case law has, to this day, tended to focus only on the justiciability of public interest and not its meaning.[62] Further, the President has not delegated the power to revoke.[63] Under the **National Land Policy** the President shall retain the power of revocation.[64]

2.2.4 The holder of a Right of Occupancy holds subject to such conditions,[65] express (usually in the Certificate of Occupancy) or implied by law (principally, under the **Land Ordinance**;[66] the Land Regulations, 1948; the **Land (Law**

of Property and Conveyancing) Ordinance;[67] the **Land Registration Ordinance**;[68] the **Town and Country Planning Ordinance**; and, **Township (Building) Rules** [69]).

2.2.5 It is important to note that under section 2(1) of the **Land (Law of Property and Conveyancing) Ordinance**, the law relating to real property in force in England on 1 January 1922 shall apply to real property in the Territory in like manner as it applies to real property in England and the English law and practice of conveyancing in force in England on the day aforesaid shall be in force in the Territory. The foregoing provision comprises what has come to be known as "Special Reception".[70] But such English law shall be in force so far only as the circumstances of the Territory and its inhabitants, and the limits of her Majesty's jurisdiction permit.[71] When such English law or practice is inconsistent with any provision contained in any Ordinance or other legislative act or Indian Act[72] for the time being in force in the Territory, such last mentioned provision shall prevail.[73]

2.2.6 Unlike the **Land Ordinance**, the **Land Act**, 1999, from section 25 through 35, contains more detailed provision concerning the grant and incidents of a Right of Occupancy. The Act prescribes the procedure of applying for a Right Occupancy,[74] determination of the application by the Commissioner for Lands,[75] issuance (by the Commissioner to the applicant) of a Letter of Offer of Right of Occupancy,[76] acceptance of the offer, [77] the grant itself and issuance of Certificate of Occupancy to the applicant [78]and registration of the Letter of Offer where the Certificate aforesaid is not issued within 180 days of the receipt acceptance of the offer by the Commissioner.[79]

2.2.7 The comprehensive structure of the **Land Act**, 1999, which in large measure is attributable to the desire for transparency, appears to be aimed against the malpractice and inefficiency brought about by the exploitation of loopholes and gaps in current legislation.[80] A classical example of such malpractice and inefficiency is the incident of "double-allocation", which has seen one plot being allocated to two persons under distinct titles.[81] The mandatory provisions for transparency under the **Land Act**, 1999 might possibly offer the long awaited disincentive to malpractice and inefficiency in land administration.

2.2.8 Like the **Land Ordinance**, the **Land Act**, 1999, under section 32 (1)(a), provides that a Right of Occupancy shall be granted for a term of up to but not exceeding 99 years. Short Term Rights of Occupancy, not exceeding 4 years and Rights of Occupancy from year to year, will also be available under the Act.[82] But, as is now the case, only Long Term Rights of Occupancy shall be subject to compulsory registration.[83]

2.2.9 Under the **Land Ordinance**, except with the approval of the President, no single Right of Occupancy shall be granted to a non-native in respect of any area of land exceeding 5,000 acres.[84] Under the **Land Act**, 1999,[85] an application for a Right of Occupancy shall, if made by a non-citizen, be accompanied by a Certificate of Approval granted by the Tanzania Investment Center under the **Tanzania Investment Act**, 1967[86] and any other documentation which may be prescribed by that Act or any other law.

---

[26] Defined as a relation or association between one person (or persons) on the one hand and another person (or persons) on the other hand, based on confidence, by which property is vested in or held by the one person, on behalf of and for the benefit of another. The holder of the property is the trustee, and the beneficial owner is the *cestui que trust*. A "*cestui que trust*" is the Latin for beneficiary. See P.G. Osborn, **A Concise Law Dictionary for Students and Practitioners**, op. cit., at p. 65.

[27] That is to say the *cestui que trust*. "Beneficial owner" is defined in Osborn, **A Concise Law Dictionary for Students and Practitioners**, op. cit., at p. 47, as the person who enjoys or who is entitled to the benefit of property. In Steven H. Gifis, **Law Dictionary**, Second Edition (New York: Barron's Educational Series, Inc., 1984) p. 44, " beneficial use" with respect to property, is defined as the right to its full and profitable enjoyment as exists where legal title is in one person while right to such use or interest is in another. Compare with "usufruct" under footnote 46,

infra. For a fairly recent examination, by the Court of Appeal of Tanzania, of the concept "public land"; the history and incidents of a Right of Occupancy; and; a Right of Occupancy as private property see the case of *The Hon. Attorney General v. Lohay Akonaay and Joseph Lohay* (1994), Civil Appeal No. 31 of 1994 (unreported), pp. 7 to 13.

[28] See, for example, **Report of the Presidential Commission of Inquiry Into Land Matters**, op. cit., p.13, paras 16 through 21for an incisive discussion into the matter.

[29] Specifically, para 4.1.1 (i) and (ii) at p. 9 of the **National Land Policy**, op. cit.

[30] See, for example, the entire para 4.2 at pp. 10 through 21 of the **National Land Policy**, op. cit.

[31] Article 24 of the **Constitution of the United Republic of Tanzania**, 1977 already provides that, subject to the relevant laws of the land, every person has the right to own or hold any property lawfully acquired. That a person shall not arbitrarily deprived of his property for the purpose of acquisition or any other purpose without the authority of the law, which shall set out conditions for fair and adequate compensation.

[32] Section 3(1)(f) and (j) of the **Land Act**, 1999 provide, *inter alia*, that among the Fundamental Principles which shall guide interpretation of that Act is that an interest in land has value and such value is taken into consideration in any transaction affecting that interest, and to facilitate the operation of a market in land.

[33] Section 3(1)(g) of the **Land Act**, 1999. Currently, acquisition of Right of Occupancy and compensation therefor, are governed by sections 3, 4 and 11 of the **Land Acquisition Act**, 1967, Act No. 47 of 1967.

[34] Section 3(1) of the **Land Act**, 1999.

[35] See, for example, paragraphs 2.5 and 2.6, at page 5 of the **National Land Policy**.

[36] See, for example, paragraph 8.2.1 at page 41 of the **National Land Policy**.

[37] Interestingly, even the **National Land Policy**, after stating that an Allocating Authority shall initiate the process of revocation if development conditions contained in a Certificate of Occupancy are not met, goes ahead to declare that "The President shall retain the power of revocation".

[38] See, for example, section 11(1) and (7), and section 14(1), (2) and (3) of the **Land Act**, 1999 under which even local authority officers are brought into the ambit of the Act.

[39] Section 8 of the **Land Act**, 1999.

[40] Section 10 of the **Land Act**, 1999.

[41] Section 12 of the **Land Act**, 1999.

[42] Section 14 of the **Land Act**, 1999.

[43] Before amendment "native", under section 2 of the **Land Ordinance**, meant "any native **of Africa** not being of European or Asiatic origin or descent and includes a Swahili but not a Somali." Upon amendment under section 4 of the **Land Laws (Miscellaneous Amendments) Act**, 1970, Act No. 28 of 1970, "native" now "means any person **who is a citizen** of the United Republic and who is not of a European or Asiatic origin or descent." (Emphasis mine.) This definition also applies to the **Land (Law of Property and Conveyancing) Ordinance**, Chapter 114 of the Laws, and in particular to section 11 thereunder. The current definition is, of course, more restrictive than the earlier one. One might in fact say that, under the **Land Ordinance**, a "native" is an indigenous Tanzanian. The Court of Appeal of Tanzania in the case

of *National Agricultural and Food Corporation v. Mulbadaw Village Council and Others* [1985] T.L.R. 88, at pp. 92 and 95 briefly examined the two definitions. The issue of indigenisation in Tanzania is discussed by Z.S. Gondwe in "Prohibition Against all Forms of Racial Discrimination: Policy, Law and Reality" in **Lesotho Law Journal**, Volume 9, 1996, Number 2, p. 13 *et seq.*

[44] *Nittin Coffee Estates Ltd and 4 Others v. United Engineering Works Ltd and Another* [1988] T.L.R. p.203 at p. 211 in which the Court of Appeal of Tanzania held that a Right of Occupancy is something in the nature of a lease and a holder of a right of Occupancy occupies the position of a sort of a lessee vis-à-vis the superior landlord. A Right of Occupancy is for a term, and is held under certain conditions. One of the conditions is that no disposition of the said right can be made without the consent of the superior landlord. An earlier judicial analysis of the nature of a Right of Occupancy was made in the case of *Premchand Nathu v. The Land Officer* [1960] E. A. 941 (P.C.), and is discussed by James, **Land Tenure and Policy in Tanzania**, op. cit., p. 134. The differences, mentioned by the Privy Council, between a lease and a Right of Occupancy include restrictions on alienation.

[45] Section 2 of the **Land Ordinance**. In the case of *Salum Mateyo v. Mohamed Mateyo* [1987] T.L.R. 111 at p.112 the High Court of Tanzania noted that under section 2 of the **Land Registration Ordinance**, Ordinance No. 36 of 1953, Cap 334 of the Laws of Tanganyika "owner" means, in relation to any estate or interest, the person for the time being in whose name that estate or interest is registered.

[46]In Osborn, **A Concise Law Dictionary for Students and Practitioners**, op. cit., at p. 326, "usufruct" is defined as the right of using and taking the fruits of something belonging to another. It was understood to be given for the life of the receiver, the usufructuary, unless a shorter period was expressed, and then it was to be restored to the owner in as good condition as when it was given except ordinary wear and tear. In Gifis, **Law Dictionary**, op. cit., p. 502, "usufruct" is defined as the right to use and enjoy property vested in another, "and to draw from the same all the profit, utility, and advantage which it may produce, provided it be without altering the substance of the thing". In the **National Land Policy**, op. cit., p.3, para 1.1, it is reiterated that "rights and title to land under any consolidated or new land law will continue to be based mainly on use and occupation."

[47] Its "deemed" character is attributable to the absence of an express grant.

[48] The **Village Land Act**, 1999, contains provision for dispositions that are governed by customary law.

[49] Section 19(1)(a) and (b). See also section 4(3) of the same Act.

[50] Most likely dropped because of its patent racial orientation as compared to the more fashionable and less restrictive "citizen".

[51] Section 2 of the **Land Act**, 1999 also defines "customary law", "customary right of occupancy", "deemed right of occupancy" and even "granted right of occupancy."

[52] See James, **Land Tenure and Policy in Tanzania**, op. cit., p. 114.

[53] The grant of Short Term Rights of Occupancy was restricted by the British Administration much earlier, under **Government Circular** No. 4 issued on 23 April 1953 by the Member (the then equivalent of "Minister") for Lands and Mines. As regards allocation of individual rights over land, paragraph 8 of the Circular stated that "The principle that a term of less than ninety-nine years is not normally conducive to the best agricultural or pastoral development was accepted by the Secretary of State in January, 1950, so that, unless there are special reasons to the contrary;

such as the prospect of land being required for African occupation after a limited period, a lesser term is not normally granted. In purely experimental areas a short-term lease of three years is sometimes granted with the option to convert to ninety-nine years upon its expiry."

[54] Ordinance No. 42 of 1956; Chapter 378 of the Laws.,

[55] This may possibly be explained by an increasing awareness amongst the citizenry that Tanzanian soil in fact has a value.

[56] Section 32(1)(c) of the **Land Act**, 1999.

[57] Section 6(2)(a) of the **Land Ordinance** permits the grant of Rights of Occupancy at will.

[58] The Court of Appeal of Tanzania has attempted to construe section 10(1) of the Land Ordinance in the case of *Patman Garments Industries Ltd. v. Tanzania Manufacturers Ltd.* [1981] TLR, p.303, from p. 308 to 310.

[59] Section 10(1)(d) of the **Land Ordinance.** One such condition has come to be known as the "development condition" under which the occupier is required to complete specified development within specified time. This condition has immediate relevance to transfer of Right of Occupancy because consent is likely to be refused if the transferor has not complied with it.

[60] Section 10(1)(f) of the **Land Ordinance**. Disposition of Right of Occupancy is governed by Regulation 3 of the **Land Regulations**, 1948. Equivalent provision under the **Land Act**, 1999 is section 45(2)(iv).

[61] Equivalent provision under the **Land Act**, 1999 is section 45(3).

[62] In *Patman Garments Industries Ltd. v. Tanzania Manufacturers Ltd.* [1981], op. cit., pp. 307 to 309, for example, in which the issue was whether the revocation of a Right of Occupancy held by the Appellant, Patman Garments Industries Ltd, over the disputed land was lawful, the Court of Appeal of Tanzania held that the function of the President under section 10 of the **Land Ordinance** cannot, even remotely, properly be categorised as being judicial or quasi judicial proceedings. Citing 3 post-reception English decisions (*Re. H.K.*, [1967] 2Q.B. 617; *Padfield v. Minister of Agriculture, Fisheries and Food*, [1968] 2Ch. 149; and, *R. v. Gaming Board, ex parte Benaim*, [1970] 2 Q.B. 417) the Court observed that "A number of eminent judges have held that such decision is no longer valid and should be abandoned." The trial judge had ventured that the function of the President under section 10(1) of the **Land Ordinance** is quasi-judicial, but that his function under section 10(2) of that Ordinance is purely executive and that he is under no duty to act judicially, that "He could throughout consider the matter from policy standpoint. I am prepared to accept that the revocation order in this case was made under subsection (2). I hold that it was a purely executive function." Apart from finding no scintilla of evidence that the revocation was under said section 10(2), the Court of Appeal held that the test in the matter is whether there is a "*lis*", that is a contest, as it were, between two sides, as between whom the President has to come to a determination after consideration of all the facts placed before him. Court was unable to see anything in the wording of section 10 of the **Land Ordinance**, which imposes on the President any duty to act judicially or quasi-judicially. But the Court of Appeal agreed with the High Court that courts have power to review administrative action which is challenged before them, it however added that such power applied to both subsection (1) and subsection (2) of the **Land Ordinance**. The High Court held that position in relation to subsection (1) alone. Indeed, the Court of Appeal held that revocation, in this

case, was unlawful and, therefore, null and void. It is illustrative that in the more recent case of *Hon. Attorney General v. Lohay Akonay and Joseph Lohay* (1994) op. cit., p. 17, the Court of Appeal of Tanzania held that "..since our Constitution is democratic, any purported ouster of jurisdiction of the ordinary courts to deal with any justiciable dispute is unconstitutional." In the case of *Kukutia Ole Pumbun v. The Hon. Attorney General*, Civil Appeal No. 32 of 1992 (unreported), the Court of Appeal of Tanzania addressed Article 30(2) of the **Constitution of the United Republic of Tanzania**, 1977, which, amongst other things, provides that no provision concerning basic rights and duties shall be construed as invalidating any existing law or prohibiting the doing of any lawful act under such law. Citing its own decision in the case *Director of Public Prosecutions v. Daudi Pete*, Criminal Appeal No. 28 of 1990 (unreported), the Court held that "..a law which seeks to limit or derogate from the basic right of the individual on grounds of public interest will be saved by Article 30(2) of the Constitution only if it satisfies two essential requirements. First such law must be lawful in the sense that it is not arbitrary. It should make adequate safeguards against arbitrary decisions, and provide effective controls against abuse by those in authority when using the law. Secondly, the limitation imposed by such law must not be more than is reasonably necessary to achieve the legitimate object. This is what is also known as the principle of proportionality." In *Director of Public Prosecutions v. Daudi Pete* op. cit., pp. 20 to 22, the Court of Appeal of Tanzania examined the scope and impact of Article 30(2) of the **Constitution of the United Republic of Tanzania**, 1977. The Ironically, the **National Land Policy**, op. cit., p. 15, para 4.2.13, notes the lack of definition of "public interest" but does not itself provide a definition.

[63] Section 49 of the **Land Act**, 1999 also reserves the power of revocation to the President. Section 48(3) of the Act, which empowers the Commissioner for Lands to recommend to the President to revoke a Right of Occupancy, enacts what previously was merely administrative practice. Another improvement over the **Land Ordinance** is section 48(1)(g)(i) of the **Land Act**, 1999, which makes express provision for the service of notice of revocation. Previously, the requirement of notice was grounded merely on judicial precedent. See, for example, the case of *Director of Land and Mines v. Sohan Singh* (1952) 1 T.L.R 631. See also James, **Land Tenure and Policy in Tanzania**, op. cit., and pp. 131 and 132. In the more recent case of *Rajabu Hasara v. Saraya Rashid* [1983] T.L.R. p111, at p. 116, the High Court of Tanzania held that the President is not legally required to cause the Land office to serve a notice to show cause why a Right of Occupancy should not be revoked. But that the court has inherent powers to look into the grounds upon which the revocation is based, and to rule whether or not such grounds constituted "good cause" for the Land Office to move the President to revoke a Right. Suffice it to say that the requirement of notice is grounded in the principles of natural justice, and on that basis alone Court should be able to uphold or strike down a revocation. For example, in the case of *Canadian Pacific Railway v. The King* (1931) A.C. 414, which was cited in the case of *Director of Land and Mines v. Sohan Singh* (1952) op. cit., it was held that a license could be revoked only by notice determining it upon a future date as would give the licensee sufficient time not only to remove his improvements but also to allow for the erection of them elsewhere.

[64] **National Land Policy**, op. cit., p. 15, para 4.2.14(ii). Arguably, this prevents potential abuse of this very important power thereby enhancing security of tenure.

[65] Section 9(1) of the **Land Ordinance**.
[66] Section 21 of the **Land Ordinance.**
[67] Sections 3, 4, 5, 7, 8, 9, 15, 16 and, especially, sections 2 (application of English law), 11 (dealings in land between natives and non-natives) and 13 (powers of bodies corporate to hold land) of that Ordinance. Once the **Land Act**, 1999 becomes operational, the holder of a Right of Occupancy will hold subject to the provisions of that Act and not of the **Land Ordinance** or of the **Land (Law of Property and Conveyancing) Ordinance.**
[68] In relation to this work, of most immediate relevance are PART III (grant of public land), PART VI (dispositions) and PART XIII (execution of deeds) of that Ordinance.
[69] Government Notice No. 48 of 1931. The Rules were made under section 3 of the **Townships Ordinance**, Ordinance No. 10 of 1920, Chapter 101 of the Laws (Repealed). The Ordinance was repealed under section 3 of the **Laws Revision (Miscellaneous Repeals) Act**, 1994,Act No. 8 of 1994, but the repealing Act is silent on the fate of the Rules. Under section 15 of the **Interpretation of Laws and General Clauses Act**, 1972, Act No. 30 of 1972, Chapter 1 of the Laws, where any Act or part of an Act is repealed and re-enacted by another Act, subsidiary legislation made under the Act or part of the Act so repealed shall, unless a contrary intention appears, remain in force, so far as it is not inconsistent with the provisions of the repealing Act, until such subsidiary legislation made under the Act or part of the Act so re-enacted, and until such revocation shall be deemed to have been lawfully done under the provisions so re-enacted. Under section 3(1) of the **Interpretation of Laws and General Clauses Act**, 1972, "Act" also means an Ordinance. Provisions under the Townships Ordinance have, substantially, been re-enacted under the **Local Government (Urban Authorities) Act**, 1982, Act No. 7 of 1982, but the **Township (Building) Rules** have not been revoked under that, or any other, Act.
[70] As opposed to "General Reception" under section 2(2) of the **Judicature and Application of Laws Ordinance**, Ordinance No 57 of 1961, Chapter 453 of the Laws, which enjoins the High Court of Tanzania to exercise its jurisdiction in conformity with the substance of the common law, the doctrines of equity and the statutes of general application in force in England on 22 July 1920 so far as the circumstances of Tanganyika and its inhabitants permit, and subject to such qualifications as local circumstances may render necessary. See G. F. A. Sawyer and J. A. Hiller, **The Doctrine of Precedent in the Court of Appeal for East Africa** (Dar es Salaam: Tanzania Publishing House, 1971) pp.15 to 23 for a discussion concerning "General Reception" and "Special Reception".
[71] Section 2(2) of the **Land (Law of Property and Conveyancing) Ordinance.**
[72] Under sections 2 and 3 of the **Indian Acts (Application) Ordinance**, Ordinance No. 7 of 1920, Chapter 2 of the Laws, among the Indian Acts then applied to Tanganyika were the **Indian Penal Code**; the **Indian Criminal Procedure Code**; the **Indian Evidence Act**, 1872; the **Indian Oaths Act**; the **Hindu Wills Act**, 1870; a substantial portion of the **Indian Succession Act**, 1865; the **Indian Contract Act**, 1872; the **Indian Majority Act**, 1875; the **Indian Probate and Administration Act**, 1881; and, the **Indian Limitation Act**, 1908. Pursuant to section 2 of the **Penal Code**, Ordinance No. 11 of 1930, Chapter 16 of the Laws, the **Indian Penal Code** ceased to apply to Tanganyika as from 1 July 1930. Likewise, pursuant to section 354 of the **Criminal Procedure Code**, Ordinance No 5 of 1945, Chapter

20 of the Laws (now repealed), the **Indian Criminal Procedure Code**, 1908 ceased to apply to Tanganyika as from 1 July 1930. Section 98 of the **Civil Procedure Code**, 1966 Act No. 49 of 1966 disapplied the **Indian Code of Civil Procedure**. The **Evidence Act**, 1967, Act No 48 of 1967, in Note (4) under section 180, disapplied the **Indian Evidence Act**, 1872. The **Indian Limitation Act**, 1908 has been disapplied under section 47 of the **Law of Limitation Act**, 1971, Act No. 10 of 1971, while the **Indian Probate and Administration Act**, 1881 has been repealed under section 141(1) of the **Probate and Administration Ordinance**, Ordinance No. 35 of 1961, Chapter 445 of the Laws, more specifically under the First Part of the Third Schedule to that Ordinance. The **Indian Contract Act**, 1872 has been repealed under section 227(1) of the Law of Contract Ordinance, Ordinance No. 1 of 1961, Chapter 433 of the Laws. Of the Indian Acts mentioned here, only the **Hindu Wills Act**, 1870 and the **Indian Succession Act**, 1865 are still in the statute book. Of course, provisions under the disapplied Indian Acts have been re-enacted, in most cases verbatim, under local legislation. Indeed, under section 11(6) of the **Revised Laws and Annual Revision Ordinance**, Ordinance No. 5 of 1955, Chapter 356 of the Laws, in the preparation of the Revised Laws and each annual supplement the Attorney-General shall have the power to transfer any provision contained in an enactment from that enactment to any other enactment to which it more properly belongs.

[73] Section 2(3) of the **Land (Law of Property and Conveyancing) Ordinance.**

[74] Section 25 of the **Land Act**, 1999.

[75] Section 26 of the **Land Act**, 1999.

[76] Section 27 of the **Land Act**, 1999.

[77] Section 28 of the **Land Act**, 1999.

[78] Section 29 of the **Land Act**, 1999.

[79] Originates from the **National Land Policy**, op. cit., pp. 18 and 19, para 4.2.22(i). Now, section 30 of the **Land Act**, 1999. The Letter of Offer shall first be registered under the **Registration of Documents Ordinance**, Ordinance No. 13 of 1923, Chapter 117 of the Laws, and shall then, under section 27 of the **Land Registration Ordinance**, be delivered to the Registrar of Titles for registration as if it were a Certificate of Occupancy whereupon registration under the **Registration of Documents Ordinance** shall cease.

[80] See, for example, the **Clause-by Clause Commentary, A Draft Bill for the Land Act**, prepared for the then Ministry of Lands, Housing and Urban Development, United Republic of Tanzania under an ODA Contract, para 11.1, at p. 61, where it is stated, with reference to Part IX of A **Draft Bill for the Land Act, Arrangement of Clauses** (Part VIII of the **Land Act**, 1999) that "This Part is designed 57 to create a clear statutory framework for the making of dispositions affecting land."

[81] This very undesirable incident is discussed in Z.S. Gondwe, "Legislative Comprehensiveness-An Assessment of Two Tanzanian Provisions" in **Law and Politics in Africa and Asia and Latin America**, 1. Quartal 1985, p. 37 *et seq.*

[82] Section 32 (1)(c) of the **Land Act**, 1999.

[83] Section 27 of the **Land Registration Ordinance.**

[84] Section 17 of the **Land Ordinance**.

[85] Section 25 (1)(h) of the **Land Act**, 1999

[86] Act No. 7 of 1997.

CHAPTER THREE

TRANSFER OF A RIGHT OF OCCUPANCY

3.1 The Character of a Transfer of a Right of Occupancy

3.1.1 None of the relevant legislation has defined "transfer". Elsewhere the term has been defined as to convey from one place, person etc., to another; specifically, to make over the possession or control of (as to transfer a title to land); sell or gift. An **act of the parties** or **of the law**, by which the title to property is conveyed from one person to another.[87] At another place "transfer" has been defined as the passage of a right from one person to another (i) by virtue of an act done by the transferor with that intention, as in the case of a conveyance or an assignment by way of sale or gift etc., or (ii) by operation of law, as in the case of forfeiture, bankruptcy, descent or intestacy. A transfer may be absolute or conditional as by way of security. [88] At yet another place, it is said that to "transfer" is to convey or remove from one person or place to another; to sell or give; specifically, to take over possession or control as in the transfer of title to land.[89]

3.1.2 An "assignment" is the transfer of an interest in a right or property from one party to another.[90] To "convey" in the law of real property is to transfer property from one person to another; in its widest sense, it means the transfer of property from one person to another by means of a **written instrument** and **other formalities**.[91] "Transfer", as shall be discussed in this work, is the transmission of a Right of Occupancy from one person to another by an act of the parties as effected by sale or gift, and not by operation of law or by a will.

3.1.3 "Transfer", as observed earlier, includes the passage of a right from one person to another by virtue of an act done by the transferor with that intention, as in the case of a conveyance or an assignment by way of "sale". Indeed, "sale" is said to be a transfer of a right of property in consideration of a sum of money.[92] This is precisely what the form prescribed for transfer of Right of Occupancy under the **Land Registration Ordinance** says.[93]

3.1.4 Elsewhere, "sale" is said to be a contract or agreement by which property is transferred from the seller [vendor] to the buyer [vendee] for a fixed price in money, paid or agreed to be paid by the buyer. A "sale" contemplates a free offer and acceptance, a seller and purchaser dealing at arm's length, and the fixing and payment of a purchase price.[94] In a word, it is correct to talk about "sale" of improvements situate on land, the subject matter of a Right of Occupancy. **It is also correct to talk about "sale" of the Right of Occupancy itself**, although views to the contrary have been expressed.[95] But it is not correct to talk about sale of the land *inter se* because, under both the **Land Ordinance** and the **Land Act**, 1999, the land is public. It is precisely the fact of "public land" that turns sale of a Right of Occupancy into a "conditional sale"; that is to say the validity of such sale is conditional on the approval of the public.

3.1.5 From start to finish, a transfer of a Right of Occupancy, as shown in the checklist under Part Two of this work consists of about 18 steps. Moreover, a transfer involves the persons and offices appearing in the matrix, also under Part Two, depicting the circulation of documents. A good number of problems encountered in transfer of Right of Occupancy are attributable to non-observance of, or ignorance concerning, such steps. The steps are, of course, derived from legislation governing transfer of Right of Occupancy. Suffice it to say that elaborate procedure and the attendant time scale is usually the price of transparency. The 18 steps may appear to be too many, but, in the name of transparency, they are desirable.

3.1.6 A "transfer"[96] of a Right of Occupancy in Tanganyika is the closest approximation to sale of land in other jurisdictions. Theoretically, because all land in Tanganyika is "Public

Land", the subject matter of the transaction are the improvements on the land and not the soil on which the improvements stand. Under section 2 of the **Land Registration Ordinance**,[97] a transfer of a Right of Occupancy is a "disposition"[98] and must, therefore, be effected by deed,[99] called a "Deed of Transfer", in the prescribed form (**Annex "A"**).[100]

3.1.7 Transfers of Short Term Rights of Occupancy are not, under the **Land Registration Ordinance**, dispositions and, while they have to be in writing,[101] they need not be by deed.[102] But the rationale for this position might have been overtaken by reality in terms of the increasing demand for this type of tenure in terms of its suitability for small businesses and its softer terms and conditions. At any rate, the Right is renewable and therefore, in terms of duration, might not differ significantly from a Right of Occupancy for a longer term. For all these reasons, in urban areas it might easily be the ideal tenure for "natives". It is time, therefore, that the exclusion of this Right from the Land Register was given a fresh look.

3.1.7 It is significant that, upon examination of the character of a transfer of a Right of Occupancy in the recent case of *Abualy Alibhai Azizi v. Bhatia Brothers Ltd* (1999),[103] the Court of Appeal of Tanzania held that the disposition of a Right of Occupancy is necessarily a tripartite transaction involving not only the holder of the Right of Occupancy and the purchaser or donee, but also involving the superior landlord (the President).

3.2 Official Search and Requisition as to Title

3.2.1 One of the least noticed provisions under the **Land Registration Ordinance** is section 3(2), which provides that the Registrar of Titles shall maintain in the land registry a land register for the registration of the title to land in Tanganyika and the recording of dispositions, transmissions and encumbrances of and over registered land. This provision flows from section 3(1) of that

Ordinance which provides that there shall be maintained at Dar es Salaam, or such other place as the Minister responsible for lands may by order declare, a land registry. Today, apart from the land registry at Dar es Salaam, there are five zonal land registries in Dodoma, Mbeya, Moshi, Mtwara and Mwanza, which, like the one at Dar es Salaam, can also register transfers of Rights of Occupancy.

3.2.2 Registration has, somewhat, tempered the force of *caveat emptor* (let the buyer beware) because every person acquiring any estate or interest in any registered land shall be deemed to have actual notice of every subsisting memorial[104] relating to such land in the land registered at the moment when he acquires such estate or interest.[105] Regardless of the substantial protection available under the registration system, a transferee would be wise to obtain information about the Right of Occupancy by way of requisition about title (**Annex "B"**) before commencement of negotiations with the transferor, and before drawing and execution of deed of transfer.

3.2.3 The transferee should also, upon payment of search fee,[106] conduct official search in the Land Registry (**Annex "C"**), by which he will obtain a summary of subsisting entries concerning the property. If it turns out, for example, that the Right of Occupancy is encumbered by a mortgage, the transferee should obtain a redemption statement from the transferor (**Annex "D"**), which will give some indication about the scope of the encumbrance. Subject to negotiation with the transferor, a discharge of the mortgage should then be obtained (**Annex "E"**). If the transfer concerns only part of mortgaged land, release of that part of the land from the mortgage should first be obtained (**Annex "F"**).

3.2.4 If the transferee agrees to pay off the mortgagee(s) as part of the consideration due under the transfer of the Right of Occupancy, he should first obtain a valuation of the property (**Annex "G"**), which the Chief Valuer, based in the Ministry of Lands, should, ideally, check and approve.[107] The parties can then draw and execute a sale agreement (**Annex "H"**).

The sale agreement is normally drawn by the transferee, and it should incorporate all the matters agreed upon.

3.13˙ Recently, the Court of Appeal of Tanzania held that a *bona fide* purchaser who is a stranger to the decree does not lose his title to the property by the subsequent reversal or modification of a decree. The Court held the view that in such a case the judgment-debtor (person adjudged to be the lawful occupier on appeal) whose property is sold is entitled only to the sale proceeds of the property.[108] Unless the transferee is willing to take an encumbered title, he should make redemption of the mortgage a precondition of his execution of the sale agreement.

3.3 The Requirement of Approval

3.3.1 Under Regulation 3 of the **Land Regulations**, 1948, a disposition[109] of Right of Occupancy **shall not be operative** unless it is in writing[110] and unless and until it is approved by the President,[111] and upon the payment of the prescribed consent fee[112] **(Annex "I")**. In addition, under section 11(1) of the **Land (Law of Property and Conveyancing) Ordinance**, a disposition of land **belonging to a native** in favour of a non-native or conferring on a non-native any rights over the land of a native **shall not be operative** unless it is in writing and unless and until it is approved by the Minister responsible for lands. Under section 11(2) of that Ordinance, the expression disposition includes transfer. Suffice it to say that individuals who happen to be non-natives and corporations, even when they are locally registered, are caught by this provision.

3.3.2 For the avoidance of doubt, a transfer by a native in favour of a non-native requires approval under both the **Land (Law of Property and Conveyancing) Ordinance** and the **Land Regulations**, 1948. That is so because approval under the **Land Regulations**, 1948 is mandatory whenever a Right of Occupancy is being transferred. A Deed of Transfer in favour of a non-native shall, therefore, if approved, bear two impression stamps signifying such approval.

3.3.3 Consent, in practice, is processed and granted by Land Officer(s) designated for that purpose by the Ministry of Lands upon submission, by the transferor, of a letter of application for consent accompanied by deed of transfer, sale agreement and Certificate of Occupancy.

3.3.4 Contrary to what Prof. James said[113] in 1971, the expression "shall not be operative" has, over the years, been subject to exactly the same vicissitudes[114] from which it was free in 1971. At that time Prof. James wrote that, apart from two East African decisions both holding the expression to mean "void *ab initio*",[115] courts have consistently held that the expression "shall not be operative" means "inoperative or ineffectual and, therefore, unenforceable until such time when consent is sought and refused or granted." This position is found in decisions of both the High Court of Tanzania[116] and the Court of Appeal of Tanzania.[117] In the former event, the transaction becomes void; in the latter it becomes valid and enforceable.[118] Most of the debate has centered on Regulation 3 of the **Land Regulations**, 1948.

3.3.5 One would, therefore, have thought that new decisions would simply fortify what appears, from the foregoing, to be settled law. But at the end of the discussion in the recent case of *Abualy Alibhai Azizi v. Bhatia Brothers Ltd.* (1999),[119] the reader is left wondering as to the state of the law on the whole issue of lack consent and its effect. In that case, the Court of Appeal of Tanzania, after reviewing an array of precedents concerning the correct interpretation of the phrase "shall not be operative", remarked that decisions both in this country and in East Africa on the matter have not been consistent, contrary to what appears to be asserted in *Nitin's* case.[120]

3.3.6 The case of *Abualy* is the latest decision and probably the most analytical in a stream of cases in the *saga* surrounding that four-word phrase, "shall not be operative". Coupled with the fact that the Full Bench (five Justices) of the highest Court of the land has handed it down, the decision shall be examined here in some detail. Two other cases having a close bearing on the case of *Abualy* shall also be examined in some detail. It is reiterated that the importance of the case of *Abualy* and the other two cases warrants this level of detail.

3.3.7 By Order dated 30 November 1999, a bench of three justices of the Court of Appeal sitting as an ordinary Court referred a matter of law for decision by the same Court sitting as a Full Bench of five justices. That Order stated that, "After discussions between the bench and the representatives of the parties, it is decided that the matter of the legal effect of lack of consent to a sale of registered land be referred for a decision by the Full Bench, as there are conflicting decisions by the Court on the issue, and that pending such decision by the Full Bench, the case is stayed and will be fixed for continuation of hearing after such decision. *Amicus Curiae* to be appointed."[121]

3.3.8 The matter referred to the Full Bench related specifically to a conflict between the decision of the Court of Appeal of Tanzania in *Nitin's* case and the decision of the same Court in the more recent case of *George Shambwe v. National Printing Co. Ltd.* (1995).[122] The conflict concerned the interpretation and application of a statutory provision requiring a contract for the sale of land to be approved or consented to by a specified public authority.[123] The provision in question was Regulation 3 of the **Land Regulations**, 1948.

3.3.9 The Appellant argued that non-compliance with that Regulation does not render a contract void, and that the words "shall not be operative" in that Regulation cannot be construed to mean void because such construction would be contrary to the express provision in section 2(2) of the **Law of Contract Ordinance**.[124] The Appellant also contended that cases decided prior to 1960 are relevant only to that period, but not thereafter, and that a transaction falling within the scope of the Regulation is **valid** notwithstanding the failure to comply with paragraph (1), (2) and (3) of that Regulation.

3.3.10 The Respondent and *Amicus Curiae* went along with the Appellant up to a point, but argued that such contract, though valid, is **inoperative** for lack of approval.[125] Court, upon examination of precedents cited by Counsel, decided that the precedents fell into three broad categories.[126]

3.3.11 The first category consists of cases in which the judicial decision is to the effect that a transaction, which does not fulfil the requisite condition, **is void in totality.**[127] The second category of cases are those in which it was decided to the effect that a transaction which does not comply with the requisite conditions **is inoperative only as to change of title**, otherwise, it is operative.[128] The third and last category of cases is that in which it was decided to the effect that a transaction which does not comply with the statutory conditions **is inoperative and unenforceable.**[129]

3.3.12 In ascertaining what it considered to be the correct interpretation of the expression "shall not be operative", the Court of Appeal of Tanzania chose to be guided by what it advanced as the two underlying principles. The first principle is explained in *Nitin's* case, that is, **a Right of Occupancy is something in the nature of a lease** and a holder of a Right of Occupancy occupies the position of a sort of lessee *vis-à-vis* the superior landlord.[130] The second principle concerns the law of contract and originates from the English common law. That principle is the principle of **sanctity of contract.**[131]

3.3.13 Guided by the two principles and by section 2(2) of the **Law of Contract Ordinance**, 1961, the Court of Appeal of Tanzania held that the expression "shall not be operative" does not mean "void" or another meaning to the same effect.[132] Court held that it means "at least that the contract in question **is valid".**[133] This is where the problem begins, how can something which is in **inoperative** be, at the same time, **valid**?

3.3.14 Court held, further, that a contract falling within the scope of Regulation 3 has all the attributes of a valid contract, **except** those performance of which, before the requisite consent is sought and obtained, would be prejudicial to the interests of the paramount landlord. That the attributes which fall within the exception, **though valid, are unenforceable** on the grounds of public policy, which protects the interests of the paramount landlord.[134] When enforcement of the contract would not prejudice the interests of the paramount landlord, a party who has performed his part of the bargain may be assisted by the court **to enforce** the contract against the defaulting party. In this fashion, a party who does not submit a written contract for consent by the specified authority may, therefore, be compelled to do so if the other party has performed his part of the bargain. But that if such consent is sought and refused, the contract becomes **wholly unenforceable, though valid**, and any expenses incurred by the parties may be recovered by legal action, if necessary.[135] Again, this statement poses great difficulty, how can a contract be **wholly unenforceable, though valid**?

3.3.15 In the manner of a conclusion, the Court of Appeal of Tanzania held that of all precedents cited to it, those falling within the second category are closer, though not completely in accord with what, in its view, is the correct position. That *Nitin's* case is bad in law since it undermines the sanctity of contract and the case of *George Shambwe v. National Printing Company* (1995) is only partly correct because it does not safeguard the interests of the paramount landlord.[136]

3.3.16 Certain aspects of the case of *Abualy* require further reflection. First, Regulation 3 unequivocally says that, without the requisite approval, a transfer is "inoperative". "Inoperative" means **not in operation** or **without effect**.[137] "Valid", on the other hand, means having legal strength or force, **executed with proper formalities**, incapable of being rightfully overthrown or set aside, as distinguished from that which exists or took place in fact or appearance, but has not the requisites to enable it to be recognized by law. **A deed, which has received all the formalities required by law, is said to be valid.**[138]

3.3.17 Under Regulation 3(1) of the **Land Regulations**, 1948, a disposition of a Right of Occupancy **shall not be operative** unless it is in writing and **unless and until it is approved** by the President. Suffice it to say that a transfer that lacks approval has still not received all the formalities required by law. Such transfer cannot, therefore, be valid. Under Regulation 3(1), a transfer that has not secured approval has already been categorised as "inoperative". So long as that Regulation is in force, there is no call to categorise such transaction further.

3.3.18 *Abualy Alibhai Azizi v. Bhatia Brothers Ltd.* (1999) also holds that, where enforcement of the contract would not prejudice interests of the paramount landlord, a party who has performed his part of the bargain may be assisted by the court **to enforce** the contract against the defaulting party. The only difficulty is, how can a contract, which is inoperative and therefore not valid, be, at the same, enforceable?[139] Can part(s) of the contract be severed from the rest and enforced?

3.3.19 Parties can draw as elaborate a contract as they want, yet, for purposes of registration, the essential terms[140] of such contract shall be those which are set out in **Annex "A"**. They consist of the identity of the **parties**, **consideration**, the undertaking to effect the **transfer**, the identity of the Right of Occupancy that forms the **subject matter** of the transfer, and **signature and attestation** of the instrument.[141] Any of these, being the essential terms of the contract, cannot be severed from it. They cannot be enforced independent of the contract because they are an integral part thereof. In a word, signature of instrument(s) or refund of purchase price cannot be enforced independent of the contract.

3.3.20 In equity, where damages would be an inadequate compensation for the breach of an agreement, the contractor may be compelled to perform what he has agreed to do by a decree of specific performance.[142] Specific performance is an equitable remedy available to an aggrieved party when the party's remedy at law is inadequate, consisting of a requirement that the party guilty of a breach of contract undertake to perform or to complete performance of his or her obligation under the contract. Unlike money damages, which are enforceable only by a judgment against property, a decree of specific performance requires that the party against whom the decree is directed **do a particular act** on pain of being imprisoned for contempt. [143] Specific performance can, therefore, be properly invoked to order a party to produce and, or, sign instrument(s) of transfer.

3.3.21 The doctrine of specific performance was examined in two recent decisions of the Court of Appeal of Tanzania. The first case is that of *J.M. Kasuka v. George Humba* (1991)[144], in which the Respondent George Humba instituted a suit alleging that the Appellant was in breach of a contract to transfer a Right of Occupancy and sought an order of specific performance compelling the Appellant to execute a Deed of Transfer. The Appellant denied ever having made such contract with the Respondent.[145]

3.3.22 The High Court of Tanzania found that the parties had in fact entered such agreement sometime before the Appellant obtained a Certificate of Occupancy over the material plot. The High Court entered judgement for the Respondent and, *inter alia*, ordered the relevant Government authorities (at Shinyanga) to effect transfer of the material Right of Occupancy to the Respondent.[146]

3.3.23 On appeal, the Court of Appeal of Tanzania was of the view that the question whether there was in fact an agreement to transfer the Right of Occupancy was ultimately one to be decided upon on the basis of the credibility of the parties and their witnesses. Court went on to find that there was such agreement between the parties upon all the essential terms and that the agreement did provide for the execution, by the Appellant, of a Deed of Transfer once he obtained the Certificate of Occupancy.[147]

3.3.24 The Court of Appeal also observed that Regulation 3(1) of the **Land Regulations**, 1948 puts contracts for the disposition of land into a special category. It avoids a contract for such disposition which is oral or which lacks the requisite approval. On that basis, Court held that the agreement was **void** because it was oral. Counsel for the Respondent proposed that Court should order the Appellant to perform the contract up to the stage of executing the Deed of Transfer so as to enable the Respondent to seek approval for the disposition. Court's response was "it is now settled law that where a disposition is inoperative by virtue of Regulation 3(1) **it is void *ab initio*** and, therefore, **all the terms of the agreement pertaining to the disposition are void and unenforceable**"[148]

3.3.25 Court, after declaring that the property was still the Appellant's, quashed the High Court's order of specific performance. But matters did not end there, the Court of Appeal, after holding that the Respondent should not be left without relief, ventured into the realm of what has greatly exercised the minds of the judiciary in Tanzania, to wit, construction of Regulation 3(1). Court held that where an agreement to sell land **is held to be void** and of no effect in terms of that Regulation, **it does not mean that the agreement is invalid for all purposes**. On the strength of two earlier decisions[149] of that Court and section 65 of the **Law of Contract Ordinance**, Court held that the Respondent was entitled to compensation for improvements effected by him on the land.[150]

3.3.26 The second case is that of *George Shambwe v. National Printing Company Ltd* (1995)[151] in which the Plaintiff, George Shambwe, sought in the High Court of Tanzania, *inter alia*, a declaratory judgement that the sale agreement between him and the Respondent for the purchase of his house was inoperative. The house was mortgaged to the National Bank of Commerce. Sometime in 1987, while the Respondent was Appellant's tenant in the house, it expressed its interest to buy the house. It was subsequently agreed that the Respondent would pay part of the purchase price of the house directly to the National Bank of Commerce towards redemption of the mortgage. The Respondent in fact paid certain sums of money to the bank, but by December 1989 the mortgage was not yet redeemed.[152]

3.3.27 The Appellant decided to redeem the mortgage himself, notifying the Respondent by letter that whatever it had already paid to the bank would be treated as rent for the period that it was in occupation of house. In the High Court, the suit instituted by the Appellant was dismissed with costs.[153]

3.3.28 On appeal, it was the view of the Court of Appeal of Tanzania that the decision of the case turned on a narrow issue; namely whether there was an agreement which was breached by the Appellant.[154] Court found that the parties had indeed reached an agreement for sale of the house. Court, however, agreed with counsel for the Appellant that, under the **Land Regulations**, 1948, the agreement was inoperative. Amongst the cases[155] cited in support of that holding is *J.M. Kasuka v. George Humba* (1991).[156]

3.3.29 Significantly, after restating the rule[157] in *Kasuka's* case, Court decided to veer away from its earlier decision, saying that the situation in the instant case was distinguishable from the earlier decision. Court observed that unlike the situation obtaining in *Kasuka's* case, in the instant case **an agreement for sale had been reached prior to seeking approval for the disposition.**[158] A rather interesting observation because it is difficult to imagine parties seeking approval before having some form of agreement in place. What will they, in such situation, be seeking approval of? Moreover, even in *Kasuka's* case an agreement for sale had been reached prior to seeking approval for the disposition. The only real difference is that the agreement in *Kasuka's* case was oral, while that in the instant case was written.

3.3.30 Proceeding on the basis of such reasoning, Court, agreeing with the High Court, went on to hold that the Appellant was in breach of the agreement even though said agreement was inoperative. Having breached that agreement, the Appellant could not invoke Regulation 3(1) of the **Land Regulations**, 1948 as a defense.[159] But the Court refrained from making an order for specific performance, saying that the Respondent had not asked for such relief. Court instead chose to leave the matter "open for further processing and execution of the documents in order to effect the transfer in terms of the law."[160]

3.3.31 The Appellant, however, had already unequivocally shown that he wanted vacant possession, and had in fact sued therefor. In such circumstances, the most viable route for the Respondent would have been a suit for specific performance. *Abualy Alibhai Azizi v. Bhatia Brothers Ltd.* (1999), as intimated earlier was decided in a bid to address this unhappy state of affairs and did so successful, until it attempted to further categorise an inoperative agreement.

3.3.32 The Court of Appeal, in both *Kasuka's* case and *Shambwe's* case, came up with justification for not making an order of specific performance.[161] The Court literally shied away from this doctrine of equity. For the record, it should be emphasized that the holding in *Kasuka's* case and *Shambwe's* case concerning the effect of lack of consent is a wrong statement of the law.[162]

3.3.33 Moreover, unless there is **express independent agreement** for refund of purchase price, **purchase price is not recoverable under some conception of "collateral contract".**[163] It will be remembered that consideration is not collateral to the contract; it is an essential term of the contract.[164] "The name "collateral contract" is not, perhaps, altogether fortunate. It suggests something that stands side by side with the main contract, springing out of it and fortifying it. But the purpose of the device usually is to enforce a promise given prior to the main contract and but for which the main contract would not have been made. They "must from their very nature be rare" and were to be "viewed with suspicion".[165] One may recover damages for breach of collateral promise or warranty if he proves such to have been given, provided always that he himself has not been guilty of culpable negligence on his part thereby disabling him from that remedy.[166]

3.3.34 However, until consent is refused, the transferee may recover purchase price under section 54 of the **Law of Contract Ordinance** if, say, the transferor refuses to sign transfer instrument(s).[167] If consent is refused, the contract becomes void and the transferee can recover purchase price under section 65 of the **Law of Contract Ordinance**.[168] More or less similar effect can be achieved under the doctrine of *Restitutio in integrum* (restoration to the original position), which is an equitable remedy in rescinding a contract or otherwise placing parties in the position they occupied before entering into the transaction.[169]

3.3.35 The general principle underlying liability in restitution is that the defendant, upon the circumstances of the case, is obliged by the ties of natural justice and equity to refund the money.[170] But this general principle is not a rule of law; therefore, in order to recover, the plaintiff must show that his case falls within one of **a limited number of categories**. For instance, he may recover if he has paid money to the defendant in pursuance of an **ineffective contract**,[171] such as a transfer that has not been approved.

3.3.36 In sum, unless and until approval is obtained, the transfer *simpliciter*[172] is inoperative. Until consent is obtained, and even if consent is refused, the transferee can obtain redress under relevant legal provisions and doctrines of equity and not, as was held in *Abualy Alibhai Azizi v. Bhatia Brothers Ltd.* (1999), through the enforcement of an inoperative contract.

3.3.37 The foregoing analysis of *Abualy Alibhai Azizi v. Bhatia Brothers Ltd.* (1999) suggests that the case has not ended the vicissitudes that have attended Regulation 3 (1) of the **Land Regulations**, 1948. It would appear, therefore, that the case of *Paschal Joseph Mlay v. Anthony Phoneas* (1968)[173] is the most accurate construction yet of the phrase "shall not be operative." In that case it was held that a distinction must be drawn between those terms of the agreement which **concern the disposition** and those which are **collateral to it** so that while the **former may be inoperative**, the **latter remain operative** and can be enforced in the event of the Commissioner failing or refusing to give consent. But the reader must be mindful of the difficulty, set out in paragraph 3.46 above, in applying the concept "collateral contract".

3.3.38 Turning to other aspects of transfer, it must be noted that all arrangements to transfer or in any way deal with Rights of Occupancy are contingent.[174] The contingency is the requirement of consent.[175] The transferee should, therefore, obtain written acknowledgment of any consideration, or part thereof, paid to the transferor (**Annex "J"**), and, if the *bona fides* of the transferor are cause for concern, lodge a caveat (**Annex "K"**). Until consent is obtained or refused it is open to either party to apply for approval of their written agreement.[176] A non-consented transaction is not made illegal by statute, collateral matters may, therefore, be enforced,[177] for example, an agreement that if consent is refused, the transferee would recover his deposit[178] and expenses incurred with interest. A person who enters possession of the premises is not a trespasser.[179] A transaction, which is inoperative, cannot be the subject of an action for damages[180] or specific performance.[181] Registration of a document not consented to because of oversight[182] does not cure the defect in the document or give it any greater validity than it would otherwise have.[183]

3.3.39 Under current law, the power to approve transfer of Right of Occupancy is discretionary. But administrative guidelines employed in the Ministry of Lands for processing approval, though not exhaustive, have proved to be of considerable practical utility. Under both current law and the **Land Act**, 1999,[184] if approval is unreasonably refused, judicial review would be available to examine the propriety of the administrative aspect(s) of such action. The reader should remember that, as pointed out in paragraphs 3.14 and 3.15 above, transfers of Rights of Occupancy to non-natives require two approvals under current law.

3.4 Stamp Duty

3.4.1 Deeds of transfer of Rights of Occupancy attract stamp duty. Under section 5(1) of the **Stamp Duty Act**, 1972,[185] every instrument executed in Tanganyika, or if executed outside Tanganyika, relates to any property in Tanganyika, shall be chargeable with duty of the amount specified or calculated in the manner specified in the Schedule to that Act[186] **(Annex "L")**. All chargeable instruments executed by any person in Tanganyika shall be stamped within 30 days of execution.[187] Likewise, every chargeable instrument executed out of Tanganyika shall be stamped within 30 days of its first arrival in Tanganyika.[188] In the absence of an agreement to the contrary, the expense for stamp duty shall be borne by, in the case of a transfer, by the grantee.[189]

3.4.2 Both the Deed of Transfer and Sale Agreement are, to varying degrees, caught by these requirements. It is provided under the **Stamp Duty Act**, 1972,[190] for example, that in any case where an agreement for sale is stamped with the *ad valorem* duty required for a conveyance, and a conveyance in pursuance of such agreement is subsequently executed, the duty on such conveyance shall be reduced by the amount of the duty paid on such agreement but shall not be less than TShs 100.00. Ideally, execution of Sale Agreement should precede execution of Deed of Transfer,[191] therefore the Deed of Transfer would be chargeable to less duty.

3.4.3 The Permanent Secretary in the Ministry of Finance appoints Stamp Duty Officers under section 4 of the Stamp Duty Act, 1972. Among public officers who have been so appointed are Internal Revenue Officers, the Assistant Commissioner for Lands, Senior Land Officers, Land Officers, the Registrar of Titles and Assistant Registrars of Titles.[192] Except as is otherwise expressly provided under the **Stamp Duty Act**, 1972, the duty with which any instrument is chargeable shall be paid, and such payment shall be indicated on such instrument, by means of a stamp or stamps in such manner as may be prescribed.[193] Usually, stamping is accomplished by use of an adhesive stamp.[194] Where any person is in doubt as to whether or not any instrument is required to be stamped or as to the amount of stamp duty payable in respect of any instrument, he may, upon payment of a fee, apply for an adjudication by a Stamp Duty Officer.[195]

3.4.4 No instrument chargeable with duty shall be admitted in evidence or shall be acted upon, **registered** or authenticated by any person or by any public officer, unless such instrument is duly stamped.[196] No disposition unless registered shall be effectual to transfer any estate in any registered land.[197]

3.5 Relevant Provisions Under the ***Land Act, 1999***

3.5.1 In as much as, under section 4(1) of the **Land Act**, 1999, all land in Tanzania shall continue to be public land even after repeal of the **Land Ordinance**, it is safe to say that, in theory, Tanzanian soil[198], that is to say the ground, will continue to be beyond sale. The **Land Registration Ordinance** and practice derived thereunder will remain in force because that Ordinance will not be repealed by the **Land Act**, 1999.

3.5.2 Dispositions, under the **Land Act**, 1999, will be governed by provisions under Sub-Part 3 of PART Vl and PART Vlll. "Disposition", as defined under section 2 of that Act, includes "any transfer". But under section 36(2) of that **Land Act**, 1999, unless otherwise provided by that Act, a disposition of a Right of Occupancy shall not require the consent of the Commissioner or an authorized officer. But the intending transferor shall send a notification in the prescribed form to the Commissioner together with payment of all dues prescribed in connection with that disposition.[199] After endorsing that notification with his signature and official seal, the Commissioner shall send or deliver it to the Registrar of Titles for registration.[200]

3.5.3 Any transfer of a Right of Occupancy which was granted to the transferor less than 3 years before the proposed transfer is to take effect shall require the approval of the Commissioner, which approval shall not be unreasonably withheld.[201] A disposition that will be carried out without first obtaining the approval of the Commissioner shall be inoperative.[202] An application for grant of approval for a disposition shall be made on a prescribed form, signed by all applicants and **accompanied by the prescribed fees**.[203]

3.5.4 The Commissioner shall grant approval accompanied by Certificate of Approval, subject to any conditions, which may be prescribed therefor, or refuse to grant approval to the application.[204] The determination whether to grant or refuse the application shall also be in a prescribed form, copied to the Registrar of Titles and delivered or sent by registered letter to the applicant.[205] If the determination of an application is not made within 60 days or such longer period as may be agreed upon between the Commissioner and parties to the proposed disposition, the approval thereto shall be deemed to have been refused.[206]

3.5.5 In short, under the **Land Act**, 1999 only transfer of a Right of Occupancy which was granted to the transferor less than 3 years before the proposed transfer is to take effect shall require the approval of the Commissioner.[207] The Act in fact empowers the Commissioner for Lands to grant approvals;[208] this is an improvement over the current situation wherein that power has merely been delegated from the President to the Commissioner for Lands.[209] The requirement of approval appears to be aimed against land speculation, and this might be fortified by the apparent transparency[210] in the whole approval process. Not least, the Act, voluminous as it is, might achieve some measure of predictability, especially for those who will be using it routinely.

3.5.6 Quite interestingly, the **Land Act**, 1999, coming in the wake of judicial precedents that have satisfactorily examined the issue of form and approval of dispositions, is not itself devoid of the vicissitudes alluded to by Prof. James. Section 36(1)(b) of the Act, for example, provides that a disposition of Right of Occupancy that does not comply with certain provisions of that Act shall be **void**. To the contrary, section 61(1) of that same Act provides that any attempt to dispose of a Right of Occupancy otherwise than in accordance with the Act shall be **ineffectual** to, *inter alia*, transfer the Right of Occupancy.

3.5.7 Such state of affairs leads to the question whether the offending transfer is downright void or merely ineffectual. If merely ineffectual it may be salvaged, but, if void, it is beyond salvage. This is quite reminiscent of the imbroglio that has so persistently visited the screening of dispositions in this jurisdiction. Unless this was the intended effect, the drafter(s) of the Act need to rationalise these two provisions. If that, indeed, was the intended effect, suitable amendment should be enacted to make section 61 subject to section 36(1)(b).

3.5.8 Transfer of Right of Occupancy shall have to be in prescribed form and shall not operate to transfer the Right until it has been registered under relevant law.[211] Without prejudice to provisions governing attestation and execution under the **Land Registration Ordinance** and **Registration of Documents Ordinance**, the execution of an instrument by a person shall consist of his signing it or affixing a thumbprint or other mark which shall evidence his personal acceptance of that instrument.[212] Execution of an instrument by a body corporate shall be effected in such manner as is authorised by the constitution[213] of that body or by any law for the time being in force.[214]

3.5.9 A contract for the disposition of a Right of Occupancy shall be enforceable in a proceeding only if it is in writing or there is a written memorandum of its terms, and the contract or memorandum is signed by the party against whom the contract is sought to be enforced.[215] A person may make a disposition to himself and any other person or together with any other person to himself alone.[216] The Act implies into instruments of transfer covenants which shall be enforced against the transferor his agents and persons through whom the transferor derives title other than by purchase for valuable consideration, in the same manner as if they have been expressed in the instrument.[217] One such covenant is that the transfer shall convey all rights, easements, and appurtenances belonging to the land.[218]

3.5.10 Another implied covenant is that a person obtaining a Right of Occupancy is not prejudicially affected by notice of any instrument unless it is within that person's knowledge, or would have come to his knowledge had he made such inquiries as he reasonably ought to have.[219] Notice would be imputed to such person, if it has come to the knowledge of the person's advocate or agent.[220] It is also implied that the transferor covenants with the transferee that he has the right and the power to transfer the Right of Occupancy free of all encumbrances except those to which the interest will remain subject as specified in the instrument or as is provided for by law.[221]

3.5.11 Another implied covenant is that the transferor will, at the request and expense of the transferee, do all acts and execute all documents for the better assuring of the title to the interest as the transferee may reasonably require from time to time.[222] Finally, the transferor, by implication, covenants with the transferee that all rent due under the Right of Occupancy has been paid and all covenants and conditions contained in it have been performed and observed.[223] If the transferor breaches the covenants the transfer will be voidable at the option of the transferee, and the transferee can, in addition, claim damages.[224]

3.5.12 The **Land Act**, 1999 also carries provision for the protection of creditors who might be injured by dispositions that are prejudicial to them by empowering court[225] to set aside such disposition;[226] the protection of persons receiving land under a prejudicial disposition;[227] regaining possession of the land after concluding contract for sale of Right of Occupancy;[228] relief against rescission of contract for sale of Right of Occupancy[229]and, circumstances under which transferee may seek relief against performance of the contract of transfer.[230]

3.6 Capital Gains Tax

3.6.1 Up until 1996, a transferor of a Right of Occupancy was required, under section 13 of the **Income Tax Act**, 1973[231] to pay Capital Gains Tax.[232] The tax was a charge on "capital gains income", that is to say the difference between sale price (i.e. the consideration stated in the deed of transfer) and cost of the improvements or, where the transferor had himself acquired the improvements by purchase, the price he paid therefor[233] (**Annex "M"** and **"N"**)

3.6.2 Discharge of Capital Gains Tax liability was evidenced by a Capital Gains Tax Clearance Certificate, which was issued by the Income Tax Department (**Annex "O"**). The certificate was a legal prerequisite to the registration of a transfer of a Right of Occupancy. No interest held by any person in any premises could be transferred or registered without a certificate of clearance issued by the Commissioner of Income Tax in that behalf certifying that capital gains tax had been paid or was not payable.[234] That is to say the certificate had to be obtained, and produced to the Registrar of Titles, even in cases, such as gifts made in consideration of love and affection, where no tax was due.

3.6.3 Capital Gains Tax was abolished in 1996, when, in that year, section 13 of the **Income Tax Act**, 1973 was repealed.[235] Under section 5(1)(a) of the **Tanzania Revenue Authority Act**, 1995[236], the Tanzania Revenue Authority shall administer and give effect to, amongst other laws, the **Income Tax Act**, 1973.[237] But the Income Tax Department survived these changes because, under section 16(1) of the **Tanzania Revenue Authority Act**, 1995, the Minister responsible for finance shall appoint commissioners in relation to any revenue law. But every commissioner appointed under any revenue law before the commencement of that Act shall be deemed to have been appointed under the Act.[238] In result, the office of Commissioner of Income Tax set up under section 129(1) of the **Income Tax Act**, 1973, and, therefore, the Income Tax Department, are still intact.

3.6.4 In his Budget Speech to Parliament on 10 June 1999, the Minister for Finance announced that Capital Gains Tax, which was abolished in the past, is to be reinstated at a rate of 10 percent[239]. The tax has been revived (shall be deemed to have come into operation on 1 July 1999) by the simple expedience of reintroducing[240] section 13 into the **Income Tax Act**, 1973, with two modifications. These are, firstly, the extension of the tax to sale of financial assets[241] and, secondly, a shift, in the computation of capital gains income, from **historical** cost to **adjusted** cost.[242]

3.6.5 "Capital gains income" is the difference between the value of consideration for which an interest in premises (or financial asset) is sold and the adjusted cost of the interest (or asset) as has not been claimed as deduction in respect of capital expenditure. "Adjusted cost", under section 13(2) of that Act, means the costs arrived at after adjusting for inflation and devaluation at the inflation and exchange rates applicable at the time of sale. In practice, Valuers, Quantity Surveyors and, sometimes, even accountants and auditors (**Annexes "P"** and **"Q"**) can work out such adjusted cost.

3.6.6 As was the case in the past, the tax shall not be levied where the proceeds of sale or the profits realised are income chargeable to tax under any provision of the Act.[243] Section 13 of the **Income Tax Act**, 1973 shall be deemed to have come into operation on 1 July 1999.[244] Another change to the structure of the tax is the adoption of a flat, instead of an *ad valorem*, rate. Under item 7 Head B of the Third Schedule to the **Income Tax Act**, 1973, the Capital Gains Tax rate shall be a flat ten percent of the capital gains income.[245] More likely than not, the mode of collection of the tax will replicate the procedure employed in the past, which has already been outlined above. More so because the Income Tax Department is still operational. Therefore, registration of a transfer of a Right of Occupancy will again be subject to the production of a capital gains tax clearance certificate.

3.6.7 Also noteworthy is section 119A of the **Income Tax Act**, 1999, a new provision[246] which, notwithstanding the secrecy provisions in section 132[247] of the Act, empowers the Commissioner of Income Tax from time to time to publish in the Gazette or local circulating newspapers a list of persons who have been convicted, under the Act, of any offence[248] relating to failure to comply with notice served upon him by the Commissioner;[249] making incorrect returns;[250] making fraudulent returns;[251] or obstructing an officer in the performance of his duties.[252] Under section 119A(2) of the Act, every such list may specify the name and address of the offender; such particulars of the offence as the Commissioner may think fit; the year of assessment or tax period during which the offence occurred; the amount or estimated amount of the tax or additional tax involved and the particulars of the fine or sentence imposed. This "parade of shame" is obviously intended as deterrence to would be offenders.

3.7 Value Added Tax

3.7.1 Under section 19 of the **Value Added Tax Act**, 1997,[253] any person whose taxable (i.e., before tax) turnover exceeds, or the person has reason to believe will exceed, TShs. 20,000,000.00 over a twelve months period shall, effective 1 January 1998, make application in the **prescribed form** to be registered within 30 days of becoming liable to make such application. The Commissioner for Value Added Tax shall maintain a register in which he shall record such particulars of the taxable persons and their businesses and any other information he may require from taxable persons when applying for registration,[254] and shall issue a taxable person registered under the Act[255] with a Certificate of Registration. In fact under section 2 of the Act, "taxable person" means person registered or required to be registered under the provisions of the Act.

3.7.1 Value Added Tax (**VAT**) is charged on the supply of goods and services in Mainland Tanzania on and after 1 July 1998.[256] VAT is charged on any supply of goods or services in Mainland Tanzania where it is a taxable supply made by a taxable person in the course of or in furtherance of any business carried on by him, and shall be payable by a taxable person at the end of a prescribed accounting period or at any time which the Commissioner for Value Added Tax may prescribe.[257] Although VAT is collected from a taxable person, in point of fact the recipient of goods or services supplied by the taxable person pays it. Indeed, a "taxable supply" means any supply of goods or services made by a taxable person in the course of or in furtherance of his business.[258]

3.7.2 Under section 4(4) of the **Value Added Tax Act**, 1997, anything which is not a supply of goods, but is done for a consideration, including the (granting or) assignment of any right is a supply of services. In other words, a transfer, by a taxable person, of a Right of Occupancy for consideration is a taxable supply of services. VAT is charged at the rate of 20% of the taxable value,[259]and, though required to be remitted to the authorities by the transferor, is in fact paid by the transferee. The value, on which VAT is charged on as a taxable supply, where a supply is for monetary consideration, is the amount of the consideration excluding VAT.[260] In practice, therefore, VAT is chargeable on the consideration declared, by a taxable person, in the Deed of Transfer of Right of Occupancy. VAT may be recovered as civil debt, in the court of a Resident Magistrate, at the instance of the Commissioner-General of the Tanzania Revenue Authority.[261]

3.7.3 It is important to remember that only transfers by taxable person(s) are chargeable with VAT. Estate agents are likely to be ready candidates for VAT. Ironically, transfers by non-taxable persons, regardless of frequency, will not trigger the charge. The law should quickly be amended to plug the loophole and remove this obvious inequity.

3.8 Land Rent

3.8.1 No disposition shall be registered unless there is furnished to the Registrar of Titles a certificate in writing by the Commissioner for Land Rent signifying his approval to the disposition[262] The form used in the past for this purpose appears as **Annex "R"** hereto. This is yet another provision that has lagged behind reality because, following the repeal of the **Land Rent and Service Charges Act**, 1974,[263] the charge is now collected by the Ministry of Lands whose Chief Account simply signifies payment of land rent, quoting relevant exchequer receipts, by letter. In the name of transparency, it is recommended that the form should be re-introduced, with the necessary modifications of course. It will be recalled that no disposition unless registered shall be effectual to transfer any estate in any registered land. It should also be borne in mind that no disposition shall be registered unless it satisfies the requirements of any other relevant law.[264]

3.9 License to Hold Land by Body Corporate

3.9.1 For example, under section 13(1) of the **Land (Law of Property and Conveyancing) Ordinance**,[265] a body corporate which is incorporated outside Tanganyika and which does not hold a Certificate of Compliance issued by the Registrar of Companies in Tanganyika can only hold a Right of Occupancy after it obtains a **license to hold land by a body corporate**. It is, therefore, advisable that a transferee body corporate should process such license simultaneously with the approvals mentioned in paragraph 3.14, above, otherwise the attendant disposition might not be registered.

3.9.2 section 183, repeal the **Land (Law of Property and Conveyancing) Ordinance** thereby abolishing the license and also the requirement of additional approval for transfers by natives in favour of corporations, which is mentioned in paragraphs 3.14 and 3.52 above. But such bodies will still have to show that they require the land for purposes of investment prescribed under the **Tanzania Investment Act**, 1997.[266] This, compared with the current position, might make land less accessible to foreigners in terms of actual grants of Rights of Occupancy.[267] But it must be borne in mind that the requirement might be circumvented by the simple expedience of a long lease given by the holder of a granted, or even deemed, Right of Occupancy to a foreigner. Leases to foreigners may, therefore, have to be subjected to the same requirement if the intention is to insure that all land held by them is held for purposes of investment prescribed under the **Tanzania Investment Act**, 1997.

3.10 Registration

3.10.1 In practice, application for registration (**Annex "S"**) is normally done by the transferee, and is accompanied, amongst other things, by the deed of transfer as approved and Certificate of Occupancy. If it appears to the Registrar of Titles that any deed presented for registration is improper in form or in substance or is otherwise expressed in a manner inconsistent with the principles on which the land register is to be kept, he may refuse registration, either absolutely or subject only to such modification therein as he shall approve.[268] Where any deed is expressed to be made in consideration of a sum of money, there shall be implied in the deed a receipt for such sum.[269]

3.10.2 Any person may make a transfer to himself and another person or, together with another person, to himself alone.[270] The Registrar of Titles shall retain all deeds registered by him.[271] Indeed, except where it is otherwise provided, all deeds, applications and other documents on which any entry in the Land Register is founded are retained in the

Land Registry and may not be taken away without a written order of the Registrar or an order of the High Court.[272] Therefore parties who desire to retain, after registration, copies of instrument(s) so registered have to present to the Registrar a sufficient number of copies of such instrument(s).[273]

3.10.3 The **Land Registration Rules**, 1954[274] contain provision governing the language[275] of documents submitted for registration; size and quality of paper to be used; prescribed forms; authorised witnesses;[276] attestation clauses; and, Filed Document number(s).[277] The transferee should see that all instruments evidencing the transfer are executed by all necessary parties and properly attested. Where execution is by attorney under a power not made irrevocable, the purchaser should satisfy himself that the power has not been revoked.[278]

3.10.4 Should the holder of two or more contiguous Rights of Occupancy desire to combine said contiguous parcels of land and **transfer** them as one parcel,[279] the Registrar of Titles may upon application by such holder in the prescribed form made with the consent of the Commissioner for Lands combine such parcels by canceling the folios of the Land Register relating thereto and preparing a new folio or folios in respect of the parcel resulting from such combination[280] (**Annex "T"**).

3.10.5 Likewise, should the holder of a Right of Occupancy wish to divide his land with a view to transferring some or all of the resulting portions, the Registrar may on the application of such holder with the consent of the Commissioner for Lands divide such parcel into two or more parcels by canceling the folio or folios of the Land Register relating thereto and preparing new folios in respect of the new parcels[281] (**Annex "U"**). But if the Right of Occupancy is subject to a Mortgage, the parcel shall not be divided unless the consent in writing of the lender (mortgagee) is first produced to the Registrar.[282]

3.10.6 For the avoidance of doubt, the Registrar may effect the combination of any parcels, or the division of a parcel, whether or not any such parcel is subject to a lease.[283]

3.10.7 Under section 2(1) of the **Land Registration Ordinance** "reparcellation" means the alteration of the boundaries of two or more contiguous parcels to form new parcels differing in area or lay-out. Under the same provision, a "parcel" is an area of registered land (such as a Right of Occupancy). Where a transfer calls for reparcellation of contiguous Rights of Occupancy, the Registrar may, subject to the consent of all persons interested in such parcels and subject to the consent of the Commissioner for Lands, cancel the folios of the Land Register relating to such parcels and prepare new folios in accordance with the revised layout[284] (**Annex "V"**). But, if in the opinion of the Registrar a proposed reparcellation involves substantial changes of ownership which should be effected by ordinary transfers, he may, in his absolute discretion, refuse to effect such reparcellation.[285]

3.10.8 No transfer of a Right of Occupancy (whether arising out of the division discussed in paragraph 3.87 above, or reparcellation) shall be registered unless the division thereof is made vertically.[286] This is because registration of estates, as it now exists, is largely pegged to the index map. Under section 86(1) of the **Land Registration Ordinance**, the Registrar shall keep an index map **showing boundaries** of all registered land and containing such other information as the Registrar shall determine.[287] Obviously, this map can only make sense if division of registered land is made vertically, otherwise the boundaries shown thereon and the whole essence of registration will be rendered meaningless.

3.10.9 No deed of transfer of Right of Occupancy shall be registered unless executed by all persons who are parties thereto and attested (**Annex "W"**) in accordance with the provisions[288] of the **Land Registration Ordinance**. But the Registrar may for good cause dispense with the signature of a transferee (buyer).[289] Registration of the several incidents examined heretofore is attended by the payment of registration fees (**Annex "X"**). Examination of **Annex "X"** will show that the fees chargeable thereunder are a pittance. Indeed, in practice, the **minimum** fees charged for the registration of any memorial is TShs. 1,000/=. Regrettably, this practice lacks statutory justification. Logic demands that the fees, fixed in 1954, should, at the very least, be revised to reflect the current value of the much-depreciated Tanzanian Shilling.

3.10.10A transfer triggers seven levies, which are: search fee; consent fee; stamp duty; capital gains tax; value added tax; land rent; and, registration fees. Apart from capital gains tax and valued added tax, the remaining six levies are collected by the Ministry of Lands and its authorised agents or agents of the Commissioner for Lands, such as the Land Registry. The transfer process would certainly be shortened if the Land Registry collected all eight levies; amounts due to other authorities could then be relayed to them.

3.10.11Provision under the **Land Registration Ordinance** governing dispositions are complemented by the **Land Act**, 1999 in that every instrument effecting any disposition under the Act will have to use the prescribed forms specified in relation to that disposition under that Act or any other written law.[290] Moreover, no instrument effecting any disposition under that Act shall operate to transfer a Right of Occupancy until it has been registered in accordance with the laws relating to the registration of instruments affecting the land in respect of which the disposition is made.[291]

3.10.12An "attorney" is a person appointed by another to act in his place or to represent him[292] and a "power of attorney" is a formal instrument by which one person empowers another to represent him, or act in his stead for certain purposes.[293] In general the capacity to appoint agents is coincident with capacity to contract.[294] A power of attorney is construed strictly, and should, therefore, mention in express words any power which it is intended to confer.[295] A power of attorney may be either general, as in the authorisation to sell property, or specific, as in the authorisation to sell to a particular person.[296] A deed executed in pursuance of such a power is properly executed in the name of the donor or with words to show that the attorney is signing for him.

3.10.13 The donor of a power of attorney may, however, by the authority of the donor of the power, and if the donee thinks fit, execute or do any assurance, instrument or thing in and with his own name and signature, and under his own seal, when sealing is required.[297] The Registrar shall, on the joint application of the donor (transferor or transferee) and the donee of a Power of Attorney, which contains any power to transfer a Right of Occupancy, file such Power of Attorney (**Annex "Y"**).[298]

3.10.14 A transfer of a Right of Occupancy may be in consideration of "natural love and affection" (a gift). In order for the agreement evidencing the transfer to be a valid contract it must be in writing and must be registered under the **Registration of Documents Ordinance**[299] will be valid.[300] Such transfer is a 'disposition" within the definition of that term under both the **Land Regulations,** 1948 and the **Land Registration Ordinance** and must, therefore, **even for capital gains tax requirements**, be processed in the same way as a regular transfer. This will entail the preparation and submission of regular documents of transfer. Yet, being a gift, the transfer is not for valuable consideration, it is only for "good" consideration, which is valid in law.[301] Such transfer will not yield capital gain income, thereby precluding the imposition of capital gains tax.[302] Nevertheless, the donor of the gift and the donee are normally required by land and tax officials to substantiate, by documents and otherwise, the basis of "natural love and affection". Suffice it to say that parent/child, spouse/spouse or relation/relation gifts should readily pass muster.

3.11 Other Relevant Considerations

3.11.1 The advent of the **Land Act**, 1999, in addition to repeal of the **Land Ordinance** and the **Land (Law of Property and Conveyancing) Ordinance,** promises some other interesting prospects. For example, at present, so far as the circumstances of the territory and its inhabitants permit, the English law and practice of conveyancing in force in England on 1 January 1922 shall be in force in the territory.[303] Under the **Land Act**, 1999, the law to be applied by the Courts in implementing, interpreting and applying that Act is the **customary law** of Tanzania and **the substance of the common law and the doctrines of equity as applied from time to time in any other countries of the Commonwealth** which appear to the Courts to be relevant to the circumstances of Tanzania.[304]

3.11.2 Practical transitional provision is contained in section 185 (2) of the **Land Act**, 1999, which will provide that subject to the provisions of that Act and until they are repealed or amended, the conditions contained in the **Land Regulations,** 1948 as amended from time to time shall, unless they are specifically excluded or repealed or rendered of no effect by any of the provisions of that Act, continue to apply to any Right of Occupancy that will be granted under that Act. All these prospects appear to be in furtherance of "endeavors to create a common law of Tanzania applicable in equal measure to all land".[305]

3.11.3 Because of its anticipatory nature, an option to "purchase"[306] is not a disposition under the **Land Registration Ordinance**, 1954. It is also not the "sale of premises"[307] contemplated under the **Income Tax Act**, 1973, because, in fact, it is not a sale. It is merely a right to demand a sale to be made. But is one of the various types of dispositions caught by the **Land Regulations**, 1948.[308] As a result, although the validity of an option to purchase is conditioned on Presidential approval, it requires neither registration[309] nor the payment of capital gains tax.[310] Consequently, it is only those document(s) (primarily, the contract containing the option to purchase) which may need to be examined as a prelude to granting approval that need to be prepared and submitted to the Commissioner for Lands for processing.[311]

[87] Henry Campbell Black, **Blacks Law Dictionary**, Sixth Edition (St. Paul: West Publishing Co., 1990) p. 1497. The same source, at the same page, also defines transfer as the assignment or conveyance of property, including an instrument or document that vests in the transferee such rights as the transferor had therein.

[88] Osborn, **Concise Law Dictionary**, op. cit., p. 316.

[89] Gifis, **Law Dictionary**, op. cit., p. 486.

[90] Gifis, **Law Dictionary**, op. cit., p. 31.

[91] Gifis, **Law Dictionary**, op. cit., p. 98.

[92] Osborn, **Concise Law Dictionary**, op. cit., p. 286.

[93] See **Annex "A"** under Part B, below.

[94]Gifis, **Law Dictionary**, op.cit., p. 420. In **Blacks Law Dictionary**, op.cit., p. 1337, "sale" is defined as a contract between two parties, called, respectively, the "seller" (or vendor) and the "buyer" (or purchaser), by which the former, in consideration of a payment of a certain price in money, transfers to the latter the **title** and the **possession** of property. It is also defined, at the same place, as a transfer of property for a fixed price in money or its equivalent. In short, "transfer", like "sale", transfers title i.e., the Right of Occupancy, and possession both of such Right and the land the subject matter thereof.

[95]See, for example, **Clause-by Clause Commentary, A Draft Bill for the Land Act**, op. cit., para 11.15, at p. 66, where it is stated, with reference to Sub-Part 3 of Part IX of A **Draft Bill for the Land Act, Arrangement of Clauses** (Sub-Part 3, Part VIII of the **Land Act**, 1999) that "Sub-Part 3 deals with the sale of a right of occupancy and concentrates on providing certain remedies where a sale goes wrong. Technically, rights of occupancy are assigned rather then (sic) sold and the parties to such a transaction are assignees and assignors but mindful of the need to write a law which can be understood by the layperson and can be translated into Kiswahili, terms more familiar to the layperson - - sale, seller and purchaser - - are used in this and subsequent parts of the Bill."

[96] Quite significantly, "assign" as defined in Osborn, **Concise Law Dictionary**, op. cit., p. 34, means "to transfer property to"

[97] Ordinance No. 36 of 1953, Cap 334 of the Laws of Tanganyika.

[98] Defined to include any act performed *inter vivos* whereby the owner of a registered estate or interest transfers that estate or interest. Pursuant to section 27 of the Ordinance, a Right of Occupancy for a term of 5 years or less is not a registered

estate.

[99] Under section 2(1) of the **Land Registration Ordinance**, a "deed" means an instrument in writing whereby a disposition is or is intended to be effected. The real distinction between deeds employed under that Ordinance and normal instruments probably lies in the fact that the former are normally Forms prescribed under the First Schedule to the **Land Registration Rules**, 1954. The Rules are made under section 114 of the Ordinance. Under section 92(a) and (c) of the **Land Registration Ordinance,** a deed shall be deemed to have been executed by a natural person or a corporation not required by law to have a common seal after such person or corporation signs and delivers it. This provision of course dispenses with the common law requirement of sealing for deeds executed by a natural person, or such corporation. But, under section 92(b) of that Ordinance, a deed executed by a corporation having a common seal must be sealed. Quite relevant here is section 6(2) of the **Land (Law of Property and Conveyancing) Ordinance**, which provides that an instrument that is expressed to be or to operate as a deed and is signed and delivered shall operate as such, and the sealing of a deed shall not be necessary. Osborn, **Concise Law Dictionary**, op. cit., p. 105 defines a "deed" as a writing or instrument written on paper or parchment, signed, sealed and delivered, to prove and testify the agreement of the parties whose deed it is, to the things contained in the deed. A deed generally consists of the following parts: the premises, the habendum, the tenendum, the reddendum, the conditions and the covenants.

[100] Section 41(1)(a) of the Ordinance.

[101] Under Regulation 3(1) of the **Land Regulations**, 1948, a "disposition" of a Right of Occupancy shall not be operative unless, amongst other things, it is in writing. The requirement of writing applies to both Short and Long Term Rights of Occupancy. In terms of evidence of the transaction, it is also advisable to reduce the transfer into writing. For example, under section of the **Evidence Act**, 1967, Act No 6 of 1967, documents must be proved by primary evidence. Section 64(1) of that Act provides that primary evidence means the document itself produced for the inspection of the Court.

[102]Even under the **Registration of Documents Ordinance**, section 8(2)(h), such disposition is not subject to compulsorily registration. In result, such disposition is relegated to optional registration under section 11 of that Ordinance. Optional registration gives rise to "constructive", as opposed to the more secure "actual", notice. A person has actual notice of all facts of which he has actual knowledge, however that knowledge is acquired; but he is not regarded as having actual notice of facts which have to his ears only in the form of vague rumours. Cases on actual notice include *Lloyd v. Banks* (1868) 3 Ch. App. 488, *Barnhart v. Greenshields* (1853) 9 Moo.P.C. 18 at 36. A person, on the other hand, has constructive notice of all facts of which he would have acquired actual notice had he made those inquiries and inspections which he ought reasonably to have made, the standard of prudence being that of men of business under similar circumstances. Cases on constructive notice include *Bailey v. Barnes* [1894] 1 Ch. 25 at 35; *Hunt v. Luck* [1902] 1 Ch. 428; *Caunce v. Caunce* [1969] 1 All E. R. 722; and, *Williams and Glyn's Bank, Ltd. v. Boland* [1981] A.C. 487. See also P. V. Baker, **Meggary's Manual of the Law of Real Property**, Fourth Edition (London: Stevens & Sons Limited, 1969), pp. 61 and 62 and J. G. Riddal, **Introduction to Land Law**, Third Edition, (London: Butterworths, 1983), pp. 72 to 74.

[103] Miscellaneous Civil Appeal No. 1 of 1999 (unreported).
[104] Under section 2(1) of the **Land Registration Ordinance**, "memorial" means any inscription in the land register, and, without prejudice to the generality of the foregoing, includes the description of any registered land, the record of the ownership thereof and the record of any encumbrance affecting the same.
[105] Section 34 of the **Land Registration Ordinance.** In the case of *Omari Yusufu v. Ahmed Abdulkadr* [1987] T.L.R.p.169, at p. 174, the Court of Appeal of Tanzania held that there is no need to undertake a historical investigation into the origins of the vendor's title beyond the inspection of the land register, because the purchaser is justified at law in the assumption that what the register contains is true and is all that there is about the property.
[106] See **Annex "X"**, *infra,* under Part Two.
[107] The office of "Chief Valuer" and, in large measure the practice of valuation itself, is not grounded on statute. For example, valuations relating to transfers in regions other than Dar es Salaam are not routinely submitted to the Chief Valuer for checking and approval simply because there is no such legal requirement.
[108] *Omari Yusufu v. Ahmed Abdulkadr* op. cit., at pp. 173 and 174.
[109] Under Regulation 3(3)(a) and (c) of the **Land Regulations**, 1948 disposition means (a) a conveyance or assignment other than by way of mortgage, or a gift, settlement, deed of partition, assent, vesting declaration, or sale in execution of an order of a court; (c) a deed or agreement or declaration of trust binding any party thereto to make any such disposition as aforesaid, including a deed or agreement entitling a party thereto to require any such disposition to made.
[110] In the case of *Nittin Coffee Estates Ltd. and 4 Others v. United Engineering Works Ltd. and Another* [1988] T.L.R. p.203 at pp. 210, the Court of Appeal of Tanzania held that an oral agreement to transfer a Right of Occupancy was inoperative and of no effect. The Court cited with approval a passage from the case of *Alexander Gray Patterson & Another v. Badrudin Mohamed Saleh Kanji &Another* (1956) E.A. 106 at p.111 that one cannot seek to enforce at law which he can only establish by a transaction declared by law to be inoperative. Court also held that the English doctrine of part performance could not mitigate the absence of writing because the Regulation in question (Regulation 3(1) of the **Land Regulations**, 1948) requires both writing and consent.
[111] Regulation 3(1) of the **Land Regulations**, 1948, G.N. No. 232 of 1948. In the case of *Farah Mohamed v. Fatuma Abdallah* [1992] p.205, at p. 210, the High Court of Tanzania held that since no consent of the President or the Commissioner for Lands or other public officer to whom the powers of the President may have been delegated, was obtained, the transfer in question was ineffective and unenforceable. In apparent reference to the Latin maxim *nemo dat qui non habet* (no one gives who possesses not), Court went on to hold that a transferee under an invalid transfer does not acquire title and, therefore, has no title to pass. Likewise, in the case of *Millen Richard v. Ayub Bakari Hoza* [1992] T.L.R. p. 385, at p. 386, the Court of Appeal of Tanzania found a transfer to be inoperative and, therefore, unenforceable because the disposition lacked consent of the Commissioner for Lands.
[112] Regulation 3 of the **Land (Fees) Regulations**, G.N. No. 191 of 1923
[113] R. W. James, **Land Tenure and Policy in Tanzania** op. cit., p. 204.
[114] "Shall not be operative" has been interpreted to mean void and unenforceable: *Chandrakant Vinubhai Patel v. Frank Lionel Marealle and Another* [1984] T.L.R. p.

231 at p. 235. In *Sylveri Mushunga v. Theonestina Rwekanika* 1974 LRT n. 30, p. 102 at p. 105 it was held, erroneously, that a contract of sale was not contemplated by Regulation 3 of the **Land Regulations**, 1948.

[115] *Fazal Kassam (Mills) Ltd. v. Abdul Nagji Kassam and Shubanu Bai Gulamhussein* [1960] E.A. 1042 (T) and *Motibhai Manji v. Khurshid Begum* (1957) E.A. 101(U), see also James, **Land Tenure and Policy in Tanzania** op. cit., p. 204.

[116] *Farah Mohamed v. Fatuma Abdallah* [1992] T.L.R. p. 205 at p. 210: no consent was obtained, therefore the transfer was adjudged to be ineffective and unenforceable.

[117] *Nittin Coffee Estates Ltd and 4 Others v. United Engineering Works Ltd. and Another* [1988] T.L.R. p.203 at pp. 210: an oral agreement to sell land held under a Right of Occupancy without consent is inoperative and of no effect because of lack of both writing and consent. This decision also corrected the error in *Sylveri Mushunga v. Theonestina Rwekanika* 1974 op. cit., by the mere expedience of pointing out that the Court in the earlier case had overlooked Regulation 3(c) of the **Land Regulations**, 1948 under which an agreement to transfer is also a disposition; *Wayani Longoi and Another v. Israel Solomon Kivuyo* [1988] T.L.R. p. 262 at p. 265: an agreement to sell a Right of Occupancy which has not received consent is inoperative and, hence, unenforceable at law. Amongst the cases cited by the Court is *Chandrakant Vinubhai Patel v. Frank Lionel Marealle and Another,* which, on this point, was not correctly decided. See also G.M. Fimbo, **Essays in Land Law in Tanzania** (Dar es Salaam: Faculty of Law, University of Dar es Salaam, 1992) pp. 127, 128; *Millen Richard v. Ayub Bakari Hoza* [1992] T.L.R. p. 385 at p.386: the contract was inoperative because the disposition lacked consent. The agreement was, therefore, unenforceable.

[118] *Mohamed Hussein Alladita v. Abdalla Bin Salim El-Harthi & Others* (1955) 22 E.A.C.A. 84 and *Patterson v. Kanji* (1956) 23 E.A.C.A. 106, see also James, **Land Tenure and Policy in Tanzania** op. cit., p. 204.

[119] Miscellaneous Civil Appeal No. 1 of 1999 (unreported), at p. 14 of the Ruling.

[120] *Nitin's* case is cited at footnote 110, supra.

[121] *Abualy Alibhai Azizi v. Bhatia Brothers Ltd.* (1999) op. cit., at p.1.

[122] Civil Appeal No. 19 of 1995.

[123] *Abualy Alibhai Azizi v. Bhatia Brothers Ltd.* (1999) op. cit., at pp. 2 and 3.

[124] *Ibid.*, at p. 5. Under section 2(2) of the **Law of Contract Ordinance,** no agreement shall be void by reason only that it is not enforceable by action under the provisions of that law for want of compliance with any such requirement or the obtaining of any such consent.

[125] *Abualy Alibhai Azizi v. Bhatia Brothers Ltd.* (1999) op. cit., at p. 6.

[126] *Ibid.*

[127] *Ibid.* In this connection, Court cited *Motibhai Manji v Khurshid Begum* (1957) op. cit., in which it was held that an agreement that had not obtained the Governor's consent was prohibited by law and was therefore void *ab initio* and *Kassam v. Kassam* (1960) op. cit. in which a mortgage of a Right of Occupancy was held to be void *ab initio* for want of writing and for want of the Governor's consent. Court noted that the two cases were decided before section 2(2) of the **Law of Contract Ordinance** came into being, but observed that a similar decision was reached in the 1984 decision of *Chandrakant Vinubhai Patel v. Frank Lionel Marealle and Another* (1984) op. cit., at footnote no. 114, *supra*.

[128] *Abualy Alibhai Azizi v. Bhatia Brothers Ltd.* (1999) op. cit., at pp. 7 to 11. Court went on to cite *Paschal Joseph Mlay v Anthony Phoneas* (1968) E.A. 563, which held that a distinction must be drawn between those terms of the agreement which concern the disposition and those which are collateral to it so that while the former may be inoperative, the latter remain operative and can be enforced in the event of the Commissioner failing or refusing to give consent. If the Commissioner merely fails to give consent it may be that a new agreement can be drawn up and resubmitted to him. Also cited was *Patterson v. Kanji* (1956) op. cit., which held that such a transaction may still be valid for some purposes although, without approval, no dealing would operate to effect a sale or mortgage or to create a charge or a sublease. The Court of Appeal remarked that this case was significant in its pronouncement to the effect that a transaction which does not comply with the requisite conditions is not totally devoid of legal effect but, "may still be valid for some purposes, e.g. if there are collateral undertakings". Another case cited by the Court in relation to this category is *Alladita v. El Harthi* (1955) op. cit., the question whether the agreement is wholly inoperative, or operative to the limited extent suggested must depend on whether its terms are severable so as to create an independent and absolute preliminary obligation to convey, which is conditional on consent. The agreement in question was, however, held to be not severable. The Court of Appeal stated that the significance of this case lay in its pronouncement to the effect that an agreement, which does not comply with the statutory conditions, may be partly inoperative and partly operative depending on the nature of the agreement. The Court of Appeal observed that the fourth case in this category, *Mushunga v. Rwekanika* (1974), although decided *per incuriam* Regulation 3, was significant in the history of relevant judicial decisions for holding that the lack of consent is only a defense to an action for specific performance or damages, but cannot be reason for holding the agreement to sell void. The last case in this category is *George Shambwe v. National Printing Company* (1995), which held that, having refused to sign the sale document thereby pre-empting the Commissioner's approval to the transaction, the Appellant was himself in breach of the sale agreement and could not resort to Regulation 3 (1) in defense. Court of Appeal observed that the significance of this case is the statement to the effect that the contract of sale was binding between the parties, notwithstanding the lack of requisite consent, but that the decision is unclear as to its effect upon the Commissioner for Lands. That if the decision meant that the binding contract between the parties obliged the Commissioner to consent to the disposition, such a decision would be wrong.

[129] *Abualy Alibhai Azizi v. Bhatia Brothers Ltd.* (1999) op. cit., at pp. 11 to 14. The first case cited in this connection is *Mohamedbhai Khanbhai & Bros v. Mtoo Binti Tafakari & Mboni* (1953) T.L.R. 43 in which it was held that the Plaintiff couldn't succeed in the absence of the Governor's approval to the transaction. The significance of this decision, according to the Court of Appeal, lies in the clarity with which it explains the helplessness of the court in providing relief to an aggrieved party. It is clear according to that case that an inoperative transaction is wholly unenforceable. Next to be cited was the case of *T.H. Patel v. L Lawrenson & Another* (1957) E.A. 249 wherein it was stated that the whole agreement was inoperative because of lack of approval and that being so that court was precluded form enforcing any part of the agreement. That it would be wrong to order specific performance up to the stage of the other party executing a transfer of the Right of Occupancy to see

whether approval could be obtained. That, in effect, would defy the law by ordering dealing without approval in pursuance of an agreement that is itself inoperative. The Court of Appeal observed that this case is the strongest voice against the enforcement of any part and any stage of a transaction, which does not comply with the statutory conditions. Also cited under this category is *Nitin's* case, which, according to the Court of Appeal, is famous, *inter alia*, because it states the principle underlying Regulation 3, that is to say no disposition of a Right of Occupancy can be made without the consent of the superior landlord. Last to be cited in this category is the case of *Wayani Longoi and Another v. Israel Solomon Kivuyo* [1988], in which it was stated that an agreement to "sell" a Right of Occupancy, if it has not received consent, is inoperative, and unenforceable at law.

[130] *Abualy Alibhai Azizi v. Bhatia Brothers Ltd.* (1999) op. cit., at p. 15. The col1orary of this principle is that a transaction for the disposition of a Right of Occupancy is necessarily a tripartite transaction involving the holder of the Right, the purchaser or donee, and the superior landlord.

[131] *Abualy Alibhai Azizi v. Bhatia Brothers Ltd.* (1999) op. cit., at p. 15. The Court of Appeal cited **Chitty's Law of Contracts**, Vol. 1, 24th Edition, p. 5, where it is stated that a concomitant of the doctrine of freedom of contract is that of sanctity of contracts; and it is still a cardinal principle of English law because it still suits the needs of a commercial community. English law is consistently reluctant to admit excuses for non-performance where there is no incapacity, no fraud (actual or constructive) or misrepresentation, and no principle of public policy prohibiting enforcement.

[132] *Abualy Alibhai Azizi v. Bhatia Brothers Ltd.* (1999) op. cit., at p. 16. The Court of Appeal was of the view that decisions coming before the enactment of the **Law of Contract Ordinance** holding that non-compliance with the requirement of approval rendered a contract void were correct only according to the law then applicable, but ceased to be precedents on the matter after 1960. (The **Law of Contract Ordinance** in fact commenced operation on 3 March 1961.) As to decisions coming thereafter but which were to the same effect as if section 2(2) of said Ordinance did not exist, Court held the view that they were made *per incuriam*.

[133] *Abualy Alibhai Azizi v. Bhatia Brothers Ltd.* (1999) op. cit., at p. 16. Court had in fact posed for itself the question: if the expression "shall not be operative" does not entail invalidity, what then does it mean? Court agreed with Appellant's submission that such valid contract has all the attributes of a valid contract (*sic*), saying that the submission was consistent with the doctrine of sanctity of contract as qualified by public policy.

[134] *Abualy Alibhai Azizi v. Bhatia Brothers Ltd.* (1999) op. cit., at p. 17. The corollary, the Court stated, is that a contact for the disposition of land, which otherwise is **proper** but for the lack of required consent, is inoperative, that is unenforceable to the extent that such enforcement is prejudicial to the interests of the paramount landlord.

[135] *Abualy Alibhai Azizi v. Bhatia Brothers Ltd.* (1999) op. cit., at p. 17.

[136] *Ibid.*, at pp. 17 and 18. The Full Bench finally direct that the ordinary Bench (three justices), before whom the appeal was pending, to be accordingly informed.

[137] **The Random House Dictionary of the English Language**, College Edition (New Delhi: Allied Publishers Private Limited) p. 687.

[138] **Black's Law Dictionary**, op. cit., p. 1550. The term also means good or sufficient

in point of law; efficacious; executed with proper formalities.
[139] See, for example, footnote no. 117 and related text.
[140] For some further insight as to what amounts to "essential terms" in contracts concerning disposition of land, see P.V. Baker, **Megarry's Manual of the Law of Real Property**, op.cit., pp. 62, 317 and 318.
[141] Elsewhere referred to as an "open contract"; see, for example, Osborn, **A Concise Law Dictionary**, op. cit., p. 229.
[142] Osborn, **A Concise Law Dictionary**, op. cit., p. 298.
[143] Gifis, **Law Dictionary**, op. cit., p. 449.
[144] Civil Appeal No. 35 of 1990 (unreported).
[145] *Ibid*., p. 1.
[146] *Ibid*., pp. 2 and 3. The High Court had found that the Appellant had undertaken to execute a Deed to facilitate the transfer of the Right once he obtained the Certificate of Occupancy, but when he did in fact obtain said Certificate he refused to execute the Deed of Transfer maintaining that the Respondent had to pay him more money first.
[147] *Ibid*., p. 5. But, unlike the High Court, which was of the view that the suit was grounded on a written agreement, the Court of Appeal found that the agreement was oral.
[148] *Ibid*., p. 7.
[149] *Peter Karanti & 48 Others v. The Attorney General & 3 Others* (1988) Civil Appeal No. 3 of 1988 (unreported) and *Nitin's* case, op. cit.
[150] *J.M. Kasuka v. George Humba* (1991) op. cit., p. 8.
[151] For citation, see footnote 122, *supra*.
[152] *George Shambwe v. National Printing Company Ltd., op. cit.*, pp. 1 and 2.
[153] *Ibid*., pp. 2 and 3. The Appellant was pressing the Respondent to vacate the house because he wanted to repair it. The Respondent was refusing to vacate the house, insisting that the Appellant should carry out his part of the bargain by effecting transfer of the house to the Respondent.
[154] *Ibid*., p. 5.
[155] The other case is *Millen Richard v. Ayub Hoza* [1992], cited at footnote 117, *supra*.
[156] *George Shambwe v. National Printing Company Ltd., op. cit.*, p. 7.
[157] That is, where a disposition is inoperative under Regulation 3(1) of the **Land Regulations**, 1948 it is void *ab initio*, therefore all the terms of the agreement are void and unenforceable.
[158] *George Shambwe v. National Printing Company Ltd., op. cit.*, pp. 8 and 9.
[159] *Ibid*., pp. 8 and 9.
[160] *Ibid*., p. 11.
[161] Compare this state of affairs with *Silveri Mushunga v. Theonestina Rwekanika* 1974, op. cit., at pp. 102 and 105 of the report, the Appellant, Silveri Mushunga, agreed to sell his house to the Respondent, Theonestina Rwekanika. It was also agreed that the purchase price would be paid in several installments. Upon paying the last installment, the Respondent asked the Appellant to go with her to the Revenue Office to sign the transfer forms in her favour. The Appellant refused maintaining that the Respondent had not performed the terms of a collateral agreement regarding payment of certain monies relating to the house and the plot. The Respondent filed an action in the District Court praying amongst other things

that the Appellant be ordered to sign the transfer forms. That Court found and entered judgement for the Respondent and ordered the Appellant to sign the transfer forms in her favour. On appeal, in upholding the judgement of the District Court, the High court of Tanzania held that "a seller cannot be heard to deny the validity of the agreement freely entered into by him by pleading lack of consent under Regulation 3 when he deliberately takes up the position wherein consent cannot be obtained." But for straying into "validity", this decision sits well with the doctrine of specific performance. But, in keeping with the doctrine of *stare decisis*, the Court of Appeal of Tanzania, being superior to the High Court of Tanzania, is not bound by decisions of the High Court.

[162] Court, in those two cases, held that where a disposition is inoperative by virtue of Regulation 3(1) **it is void *ab initio*** and, therefore, **all the terms of the agreement pertaining to the disposition are void and unenforceable**. Even the case of *Abualy* held that this was a wrong statement of the law.

[163] In Gifis, **Law Dictionary**, op. cit., at p. 77, "collateral" is defined as secondary, not of the essence of the principle thing; on the side, divergent or auxiliary. In contracts a collateral promise is one auxiliary to an integrated contractual relationship. The term may also refer to a **promise ancillary to a principal transaction**; its breach does not entitle the other party to rescind. Osborn, **A Concise Law Dictionary**, op. cit., at p. 74 says that a collateral agreement is independent of, but subordinate to, an agreement affecting the same subject matter.

[164] Under section 25 of the **Law of Contract Ordinance**, an agreement without consideration is void.

[165] G.C. Cheshire and C.H.S. Fifoot, **The Law of Contract**, Seventh Edition (London: Butterworhts, 1969), p. 54, citing *Helbut. Symons & Co. v. Buckleton*, [1913] A.C. 30 at p. 47.

[166] H.G. Beale, W.D. Bishop and M.P. Furmstone, **Contract Cases and Materials**, (London: Butterworths, 1990), p. 766, citing Denning L.J. in *Strongman (1945) Ltd. v. Sincock [1955]* 2 QB 525, Court of Appeal.

[167] Under that provision, when a contract consists of reciprocal promises, such that one of them cannot be performed, or that its performance cannot be claimed till the other has been performed, and the promisor of the promise last mentioned fails to perform, such promisor cannot claim the performance of the reciprocal promise, and must make compensation to the other party to the contract for any loss which such other party may sustain by the non-performance of the contract.

[168] Under that provision, when an agreement is discovered to be void, or when a contract becomes void, any person who has received any advantage under such agreement or contract is bound to restore it, or to make compensation for it, from the person from whom he received it.

[169] Osborn, **A Concise Law Dictionary**, op. cit., at p. 280.

[170] Lord Mansfield in *Moses v. Macferlan* (1760) 2 Burr 1005, at p. 1012.

[171] Beale, Bishop and Furmstone, **Contract Cases and Materials**, op. cit., p. 30.

[172] Defined in **Black's Law Dictionary**, op. cit., at p. 1384 to mean "by itself; by its own force, *per se*"

[173] See footnote128 *supra*, where the rule in that case is set out.

[174] Under section 31 of the **Law of Contract Ordinance**, a "contingent contract" is a contract to do or not to do something, if some event, collateral to such contract, does or does not happen.

[175] *Sylveri Mushunga v. Theonestina Rwekanika* (1974) op. cit., at p. 105.
[176] *Khanbhai v. Mtoo Tafakari* (1953) 1 T.L.R. 43; (1953) 1 T.L.R. 639 (Court of Appeal) and *National Bank of Commerce v. Manubhai Shankarbhai Desai and Others* (1969) H.C.D. no. 206 (but the interest in question in the *Desai* case was a Government Lease, and not a Right of Occupancy); see also James, **Land Tenure and Policy in Tanzania** op. cit., p. 204. Compare with *Sylveri Mushunga v. Theonestina Rwekanika* 1974 op. cit., at p. 105 where the High Court of Tanzania held that parties to an agreement of sale must take all the necessary steps to obtain such consent and a seller cannot be heard to deny the validity of the agreement freely entered into by him by pleading lack of consent under Regulation 3 of the **Land Regulations**, 1948 when he deliberately takes up the position wherein consent cannot be obtained. In the case of *Juma Sultani Mkugenzi v. Ramadhani Amin Athuman* [1991] T.L.R. p.183 at pp. 189 and 190, the High Court of Tanzania held that agreement(s) drawn shall be construed *contra preferentum* the transferor. In the instant case, the transferor failed, contrary to his own agreement, to undertake such steps as would be necessary to fulfil what his predecessor in title had agreed to do, which included delivery of an unencumbered title. The Court ordered specific performance of that agreement.
[177] *Pascal Mlay v. Phoneas* (1968) H.C.D. 1and *Gangji v. Hemedi* (1956) 23 E.A.C.A. 268; see also James, **Land Tenure and Policy in Tanzania** op. cit., p. 204.
[178] In *Sylveri Mushunga v. Theonestina Rwekanika* 1974 op. cit., at p. 105, for example, it was held that if consent is not obtained for any reason, the transferee is entitled to refund of all that he paid under the transfer, but he is not entitled to damages because it is through no fault of the transferor that he cannot convey the property. It must be pointed out, however, that the reasoning in that case would only be valid were consent is sought and refused, but would not apply where the transferor deliberately abstains from seeking consent.
[179] James, **Land Tenure and Policy in Tanzania** op. cit., p. 204, citing the English case of *Denning v. Edwards* [1961] A.C. 254 (P.C.).
[180] *Gangji v. Hemedi* (1956) 23 E.A.C.A. 268; see also James, **Land Tenure and Policy in Tanzania** op. cit., p. 204. See also *Sylveri Mushunga v. Theonestina Rwekanika* 1974 op. cit., at p. 105.
[181] *Mohamed Alladita v. El-Harthi* (1955) 22 E.A.C.A. 84 and *Bank of Commerce v. Manubhai Shankarbhai Desai and Others* (1969) H.C.D. no. 206, at p. 156; see also James, **Land Tenure and Policy in Tanzania** op. cit., p. 204. But in *Sylveri Mushunga v. Theonestina Rwekanika* 1974 op. cit., at p. 105, Court held that the transferor **must take all necessary steps** that are required before consent is sought. Suffice it to say that among the orders sought by the transferee in her action was that the transferor be ordered to sign transfer forms as prelude to seeking consent. Note that specific performance can be invoked to order a party to produce document(s) or sign instrument(s).
[182] Under section 41(1) of the **Land Registration Ordinance**, no disposition shall be registered unless it satisfies the requirements of that Ordinance and any other written law. "Other written law" includes the consent provision, that is to say, Regulation 3(1) of the **Land Regulations**, 1954.
[183] *Khanbhai v. Mtoo Tafakari* (1953) 1 T.L.R. 43, in particular the Court of Appeal at (1953) 1 T.L.R. 639; see also James, **Land Tenure and Policy in Tanzania** op. cit., p. 204. The case of *Paschal Joseph Mlay v. Anthony Phoneas* (1968), discussed at footnotes no. 128 and 173 above, would also be relevant here.
[184] Indeed, under section 41(1) of the **Land Act**, 1999, there shall be a presumption

that an application for a grant of an approval for a disposition shall be granted.
[185] Act No. 20 of 1972.
[186] Section 5(1) of the Act.
[187] Section 24 of the Act.
[188] Section 25 of the Act.
[189] Section 40 (d) of the Act.
[190] See the first proviso to Item 22 under the Schedule to the **Stamp Duty Act**, 1972, reproduced in **Annex 'L'**, *infra*.
[191] See Checklist for Transfer of Right of Occupancy under Part Two, *infra*.
[192] Paragraph 2 of the **Stamp Duty Officers (Appointment) Order**, 1974, Government Notice No. 122 of 1974.
[193] Section 17 of the **Stamp Duty Act**, 1972.
[194] See section 17 of the **Stamp Duty Act**, 1972.
[195] Section 42(1) of the **Stamp Duty Act**, 1972. As regards the procedure governing adjudication, see section 42(2) of the same Act.
[196] Section 46(1) of the **Stamp Duty Act**, 1972.
[197] Section 41(2) of the **Land Registration Ordinance**. Under section 2(1) of that Ordinance, "registered land," means land in respect of which an estate has been registered, while "estate" means, amongst other things, a Right of Occupancy. Therefore, registration of a grant of public land under section 27 of that Ordinance turns such land into "registered land", but it does not thereby cease to be public land. In the case of *Farah Mohamed v. Fatuma Abdallah* [1992] p. 205, at p. 210, the High Court of Tanzania held that under section 41(2) of the **Land Registration Ordinance,** a disposition of land which has not been registered under the Ordinance is ineffectual to transfer any title or right over it. In the case of *Stephen Kiame Sefu v. Registrar of Titles* [1988] p. 127, at pp. 128 and 129, the High Court of Tanzania examined refusal, by a Senior Assistant Registrar of Titles, to register a transfer because the transferor had not "sorted out the transfer problems with the Prime Minister's Office". The transferor had already obtained consent to the transfer. Court held that once the appropriate authority has granted approval to a transfer, the Registrar of Titles has no discretion to withhold registration unless any of the circumstances mentioned in section 42 of the **Land Registration Ordinance** actually obtains. The circumstances include any deed presented for registration which is improper in form or in substance, or is not clearly expressed, or does not indicate with sufficient precision the particular estate which it is intended to effect. The High Court also observed that under section 102(1) of the **Land Registration Ordinance,** any person who is aggrieved by a decision, order or act of the Registrar of Titles may appeal to the High Court within three months from the date of such decision, order or act, whereupon, under section 102(9) of that Ordinance, the High Court may make such order as the circumstances may require.
[198] Prof. James, in **Land Tenure Policy in Tanzania**, op. cit., p. 39 observes that to the layman "land" means any piece of ground or soil whatsoever, i.e., the physical substance. He points out that, at common law, "land" includes very much more than just the physical soil or substance. Indeed, under section 2(ii) of the **Conveyancing Act**, 1881, which applies to Tanzania by virtue of Special Reception, "land" includes land of any tenure and tenements and hereditaments corporeal and incorporeal and houses and other buildings. Section 6(i) of that Act further provides that a conveyance would be deemed to include and operate to convey, with the

land, all buildings, erections, fixtures, commons, hedges, fences attached to the soil.
[199] Section 36(3) of the **Land Act**, 1999.
[200] Section 36(4) of the **Land Act**, 1999.
[201] Section 37(2) of the **Land Act**, 1999.
[202] Section 37(5) of the **Land Act**, 1999.
[203] Section 39(1) of the **Land Act**, 1999.
[204] Section 39(5) and (6) of the **Land Act**, 1999.
[205] Section 39(7).
[206] Section 41(4) and (5).
[207] Section 37(2).
[208] Section 37(1).
[209] Item 28 under **The Transfer of Powers and Duties Consolidation Order**, 1962, G.N. No. 478 of 1962. Under Regulation 3(1) of the **Land Regulations**, 1948, the power to approve dispositions is vested, in the first instance, in the President.
[210] See, in addition, the criteria for determining application for grant of approval for disposition under section 41 of the **Land Act**, 1999.
[211] Section 62(1) and (2) of the **Land Act**, 1999.
[212] Section 63(2) of the **Land Act**, 1999.
[213] This assumes that the constitution is itself valid under relevant law, because the constitution cannot override law.
[214] Section 63(3) of the **Land Act**, 1999.
[215] Section 64(1) of the **Land Act**, 1999. This provision is reminiscent of similar provision under section 4 of the **Statute of Frauds**, 1677 of England.
[216] Section 65(1) of the **Land Act**, 1999. Provision in *pari materia* is section 52 of the **Land Registration Ordinance**.
[217] Section 66 of the **Land Act**, 1999.
[218] Section 67(a) of the **Land Act**, 1999.
[219] Section 67(b)(i) of the **Land Act**, 1999. Suffice to say that the provision covers, respectively, "actual" and "constructive" notice.
[220] Section 67(b)(ii) of the **Land Act**, 1999. As already alluded to in the text, this is "imputed notice".
[221] Section 67(c)(i) of the **Land Act**, 1999.
[222] Section 67(c)(iii) of the **Land Act**, 1999.
[223] Section 67(c)(iv) of the **Land Act**, 1999.
[224] Section 73 of the **Law of Contract Ordinance**.
[225] Under section 167 of the **Land Act**, 1999, courts which are vested with exclusive jurisdiction to hear and determine all manner of disputes, actions and proceedings concerning land include the Court of Appeal of Tanzania, the prospective Land Division of the High Court, District Land Courts and Housing Tribunals, Ward Tribunals and Village Land Councils"
[226] Sections 68, 69 and 70 of the **Land Act**, 1999. Court, under section 2 of that Act, means the fora established under section 167 of the Act, which include Ward Tribunals, Primary Land Courts, District Land Courts and the High Court.
[227] Sections 71of the **Land Act**, 1999.
[228] Sections 73 and 74 of the **Land Act**, 1999.
[229] Section 75 of the **Land Act**, 1999.

[230] Section 76 of the **Land Act**, 1999.
[231] Act No. 33 of 1973.
[232] Section 13 (1) of the **Income Tax Act**, 1973.
[233] Section 13(1) of the **Income Tax Act**, 1973.
[234] Proviso to section 13(1)(b) of the **Income Tax Act**, 1973.
[235] Repealed by section 25 of the **Finance (No. 2) Act**, 1996.
[236] Act No. 11 of 1995.
[237] The full list of laws covered by the provision is set out in the First Schedule to the Act
[238] Section 16(2) of the **Tanzania Revenue Authority Act**, 1995.
[239] The United Republic of Tanzania, **Speech by the Minister for Finance, Hon. Daniel N. Yona (MP.), Introducing to the National Assembly the Estimates for Government Revenue and Expenditure for the Financial Year 1999/2000 on 10th June, 1999** (Dar es Salaam: Government Printer, 1999), para. 57(vi) at page 53.
[240] **Finance Act**, 1999 sections 11 and 13. The amendment first appeared in **Special Bill Supplement** No. 1, dated 10 June 1999, the same day that the Minister for Finance delivered his Budget Speech to the National Assembly. For the purposes of that provision, "financial assets" are company's financial securities such as shares, stocks or bonds. But sale of shares issued by companies listed under the Dar es Salaam Stock Exchange, which at present are Tanzania Breweries Limited and Tanzania Oxygen Limited, is not caught by the provision.
[241] Section 13(1) of the **Income Tax Act**, 1973.
[242] Section 13 (1)(b) of the **Income Tax Act**, 1973.
[243] Section 13(4) of the **Income Tax Act**, 1973. Previously, this provision was contained in section 13(3) of the Act.
[244] Section 11 of the **Finance Act**, 1999.
[245] The amendment has been effected by section 21 of the **Finance Act**, 1999.
[246] The amendment has been effected by section 18 of the **Finance Act**, 1999, and shall be deemed to have come into operation on 1 July 1999. Like provision has been introduced for Value Added Tax under section 47A of the **Value Added Tax Act**, 1997, the amendment having been effected under section 34 of the **Finance Act**, 1999.
[247] The section, amongst other things, provides that every officer and every other person employed in carrying out the provisions of the Act shall regard and deal with all documents and information relating to the income of any person which may come into his possession or to his knowledge in the course of his duties as secret.
[248] In respect of offences, the publication can be effected only after any proceedings in respect of appeal from conviction have been completed, or have not been instituted within the time prescribed therefor.
[249] Section 116 of the **Income Tax Act**, 1973.
[250] Section 117 of the **Income Tax Act**, 1973.
[251] Section 118 of the **Income Tax Act**, 1973.
[252] Section 119 of the **Income Tax Act**, 1973.
[253] Act No. 24 of 1997.
[254] Section 18 of the **Value Added Tax Act**, 1997.
[255] Section 19(3) and (4) of the **Value Added Tax Act**, 1997.
[256] Section 3(1) of the **Value Added Tax Act**, 1997.

[257] Section 4(1) and (2) of the **Value Added Tax Act**, 1997.
[258] Section 60(1) of the **Value Added Tax Act**, 1997. Paragraphs (a) through (e) of that subsection gives examples of "taxable supplies".
[259] Section 8(1) of the **Value Added Tax Act**, 1997.
[260] Section 13(1)(a) **Value Added Tax Act**, 1997. Where the supply is not for a monetary consideration, or is only partly for such consideration, taxable value shall be the open market value excluding VAT.
[261] Section 31 of **Value Added Tax Act**, 1997.
[262] Section 41(1)(a) of the **Land Registration Ordinance**.
[263] Repealed under section 55 of the **Urban Authorities (Rating) Act**, 1983, Act No. 2 of 1983.
[264] Section 41(1) of the **Land Registration Ordinance**.
[265] Ordinance No. 2 of 1923, Chapter 114 of the Laws. Under section 15(2) of the **Companies Ordinance**, Ordinance No. 36 of 1931, Chapter 212 of the Laws, from the date of its incorporation in Tanzania, a company shall, *inter alia*, have power to hold land. A company incorporated outside the Territory, which has delivered to the Registrar of Companies the requisite documents for registration shall have the same power to hold land in the Territory as if it were a company incorporated under the Ordinance. In fact the "Certificate of Compliance" is issued upon registration of such documents. The Certificate does not enjoy any mention under the Ordinance, it is an administrative device albeit quite functional.
[266] Act No. 7 of 1997.
[267] Land will be granted for investment, and not for other users as is now the case. Residential use shall, therefore, have to be related to the investment in question. Seemingly, diplomatic cases will proceed on the basis of reciprocity, as is the case with other diplomatic matters.
[268] Section 42 of the **Land Registration Ordinance.**
[269] Section 46 of the **Land Registration Ordinance.**
[270] Section 52 of the **Land Registration Ordinance.** Similar provision is prescribed under section 65(1) of the **Land Act**, 1999.
[271] Section 48(1) of the **Land Registration Ordinance.**
[272] Section 98, and especially subsection (3), of the **Land Registration Ordinance.** See also **The Encyclopaedia of Forms and Precedents**, Fourth Edition, Volume 1 (London: Butterworths, 1964), para 656 at p. 329.
[273] Under section 48(2) of the **Land Registration Ordinance**, where a lease or mortgage submitted for registration in duplicate is registered, the Registrar shall endorse the duplicate and the triplicate, if any, with particulars of the registration and return them to the person who submitted them. The same logic would apply to transfers.
[274] Government Notice No. 117 of 1954.
[275] Rule 9, as amended by the **Land Registration (Amendment) Rules**, 1973, Government Notice No. 147 of 1973, provides that such documents shall be in Kiswahili or English language or in such other language as the Registrar may in his absolute discretion allow. Where any document is in a language other than Kiswahili or English there shall be furnished therewith a verified translation of the same in Kiswahili or English.
[276] Rule 11, as amended by the **Land Registration (Amendment) Rules**, 1972, Government Notice No. 89 of 1972, provides that, where the deed is executed

within Tanganyika, Kenya, Uganda or Zanzibar, the persons authorised to attest it include an Advocate, the Registrar of Titles, the Commissioner for Lands and a Land Officer. Where the deed is executed elsewhere than in Tanganyika, Kenya, Uganda or Zanzibar, the persons authorised to attest it include a Magistrate, a Notary Public and a Foreign Service Officer of the Tanzania Foreign Service

[277] Rule 4 of the **Land Registration Rules**, 1954. See also Rules 7, 10, and 12 under the same statutory instrument concerning quality of paper, prescribed forms and attestation clauses.

[278] **The Encyclopaedia of Forms and Precedents**, op.cit., para 638 at p. 322.

[279] Once in force, the provisions of sections 36 (notification) and 39 (application for approval) of the **Land Act**, 1999 shall apply to such transfer.

[280] Section 82 of the **Land Registration Ordinance**.

[281] Section 83 of the **Land Registration Ordinance.** Sections 162 and 163 of the **Land Act**, 1999 will set out detailed provision concerning partition at the instance of co-owners of Right of Occupancy. Significantly, even under the **Land Act**, 1999, applications for partition shall have to be made to the Registrar of Titles.

[282] Proviso to section 83 of the **Land Registration Ordinance**. Under the **Land Act**, 1999, such consideration will find operation under section 162(3)(j).

[283] Section 84 of the **Land Registration Ordinance**.

[284] Section 85(1) of the **Land Registration Ordinance**.

[285] Proviso to section 85(1) of the **Land Registration Ordinance**.

[286] Section 53 and the second Proviso to section 83 of the **Land Registration Ordinance**. The Report of the **Presidential Commission of Inquiry Into Land Maters**, op. cit., pp. 166 para 4 and 176 para 57, recommended the creation of horizontal tenure "whereby people can build vertically, get separate titles and thereby accommodate the interests of both the transferor and the transferee". The part dealing with land registration under the **National Land Policy**, op. cit., pp. 18 and 19, paras 4.2.21 and 4.2.22, is silent on this matter. But legislation concerning titling of horizontal division(s), otherwise called "condominium(s)", is already being contemplated. "Condominium" is individual ownership of a unit in a multi-unit structure, as an apartment building. The term also refers to a unit so owned, and a building containing condominiums. When in place, such legislation will call for corresponding amendment of the **Land Registration Ordinance**.

[287] In the case of the registration of a lease, for example, the Registrar would be perfectly justified to require the production, for registration, of a three-dimensional plan of the demised property. Much the same can be said regarding the registration of condominiums once they come into existence.

[288] Section 91 of the **Land Registration Ordinance**.

[289] Proviso to section 91 of the **Land Registration Ordinance**. At present, sections 91 and 92 of the **Land Registration Ordinance** govern the manner of execution of deeds. Section 63 of the **Land Act**, 1999 carries substantively similar provision concerning execution of instruments in writing. That is to say, execution by a person shall consist of his signing the instrument or affixing a thumbprint or other mark as evidence of his personal acceptance of the instrument. Execution by a corporate body shall be in any manner authorised by the constitution of that organisation or by any law for the time being in force.

[290] Section 62(1) of the **Land Act**, 1999.

[291] Section 62(2) of the **Land Act**, 1999.

[292] Osborn, **Concise Law Dictionary**, op. cit., p. 38.
[293] *Ibid*., p. 246.
[294] **The Encyclopaedia of Forms and Precedents**, op. cit., para 8 at p. 174 and para 20 at p. 183. The same source states that an infant cannot make a valid power of attorney. Likewise, a power of attorney executed by a person incapable through mental incapacity of understanding what is to be effected by executing the deed is invalid. A corporation, on the other hand, must act through its agents and may appoint an agent for any purpose within its capacity. But a general power of attorney in favour of one member of a firm does not confer any authority on his partners. See **The Encyclopaedia of Forms and Precedents**, op. cit., para 8(a) at p. 174, paras 8(b) and (c) at p. 175 and para 20 at p. 183.
[295] **The Encyclopaedia of Forms and Precedents**, op. cit., para 22 at p. 183.
[296] Gifis, **Law Dictionary**, op. cit., p. 355.
[297] **The Encyclopaedia of Forms and Precedents**, op.cit., para 33 at p. 195.
[298] Section 96(1) of **Land Registration 0rdinance**.
[299] Ordinance No. 14 of 1923, (Cap 117 of the Laws of Tanganyika).
[300] "Natural love and affection" is good, and therefore valid, consideration under section 25(1) of the **Law of Contract Ordinance**, Ordinance No. 1of 1961, (Cap. 433 of the Laws of Tanganyika). Under that provision an agreement without consideration is void unless it is **expressed in writing and registered under the law for the time being in force for the registration of documents**, and is made on account of natural love and affection between parties standing in a near relation to each other. Such an agreement is a contract. As regards registration of the document, the relevant provision is section 8(1)(a) of the **Registration of Documents Ordinance**. Suffice it to say that, under section 25(2) of the **Law of Contract Ordinance**, it is provided that nothing in section 25(1) shall affect the validity, as between the donor and donee, of any gift actually made. Conversely, the gift will, regardless of non-compliance with said section 25(1), be valid *inter partes*. It is interesting to note that under section 42(2)(h) of the **Land Act**, 1999, the Commissioner for Lands shall not accept the surrender of a Right of Occupancy unless it is, *inter alia*, surrendered in consideration of natural love and affection. **The provision is misconceived because "surrender" is grounded on the fact that the President holds the reversionary title to all public land, a Right of Occupancy cannot, therefore, be surrendered back to the President in consideration of natural love and affection. It is recommended that the provision should be deleted.**
[301] In the case of *Salum Mateyo v. Mohamed Mateyo* [1987] op. cit., at p.113 the High Court of Tanzania observed that the appellant had acquired title to a house by way of a gift *inter vivos* and that the issue before that Court was whether it was open for the respondent to revoke the gift when their personal relationship changed. Counsel for the appellant submitted that the gift had been unconditionally and was therefore absolute and irrevocable, but cited no authority therefor. Citing Halsbury's Laws of England 3rd Edition, Volume 18 at p. 366, Court held that it is on legal and equitable principles clear that a person *sui juris* acting freely, and with sufficient knowledge, ought to have and has power to make, in binding and effectual manner, a voluntary gift of any part of his property, whether capable or incapable of manual delivery, whether in possession or reversion, and howsoever circumstances.
[302] But the donor of the gift may still be required to obtain certification of "no tax

payable".

[303] Section 2(1) and (2) of the **Land (Law of Property and Conveyancing) Ordinance**.

[304] Section 181(1) of the **Land Act**, 1999.

[305] Section 181(3) of the **Land Act**, 1999.

[306] In Osborn, **Concise Law Dictionary**, op. cit., p. 229, "Option" is defined as "a right of choice; a right conferred by agreement to buy or not at will, property (whether land or stocks, etc.), within a certain time." It resembles a "call option", which is a **contract** giving the buyer the right to purchase **stock** at specified price within the specified time; see definition of "call" in Steven H. Gifis, **Law Dictionary**, 2nd Edn., (New York: Barrons Educational Series, Inc., 1984), p. 57.

[307] Section 13(1) of the **Income Tax Act**, 1973.

[308] Regulation 3(3)(c) of the **Land Regulations**, 1948. Likewise, under section 2 of the **Land Act**, 1999, "disposition" will include an agreement to undertake a transfer.

[309] If the subject matter of the option is a Short Term Right of Occupancy, the disposition will trigger compulsory registration under section 8(1)(a) of the **Registration of Documents Ordinance**, otherwise, under section 9 of that Ordinance, it will not be effectual to transfer said Right of Occupancy. But if the subject matter of the option is a Long Term Right of Occupancy, the document evidencing the disposition may be registered at the option of the holder under section 11 of that Ordinance.

[310] This is because the charging provision, section 13 of the **Income Tax Act**, 1973, targets actual sales, and not merely the right to require a sale to be made.

[311] Under section 39(1)(c) of the **Land Act**, 1999, an application for a grant of approval of a disposition shall be accompanied by any other information which is prescribed or which may be required by the Commissioner for Lands.

CHAPTER FOUR

RIGHTS AND DUTIES OF PARTIES BETWEEN DATE OF CONTRACT AND DATE OF COMPLETION

4.1 Date of the Contract

4.1.1 An agreement enforceable by law is a contract. [312] Every promise, or set of promises, forming the consideration for each other constitute an agreement.[313] Unless the parties state the date[314] of the contract in the contract itself, the date of the contract can be the day when the transferor promises to transfer a Right of Occupancy and the transferee promises to pay the requisite consideration for the improvements standing on the land which is the subject matter of such Right of Occupancy.[315] From the date of the contract the transferee is **in equity** the owner of the property sought to be transferred, which is held by the transferor as trustee[316] for the transferee, the transferor having a right to the purchase money, a lien on the property as security therefor and a right to retain possession of the property until the purchase money is paid.[317]

4.2 Date of Completion

4.2.1 Date of completion is the day on which a transfer of Right of Occupancy is registered, because no disposition unless registered (notwithstanding that the Presidential approval mentioned in paragraph 3.14 may have been obtained) shall be effectual to transfer any estate in any registered land.[318] Upon completion, it is good practice for the parties, especially if they have legal representation, to draw a completion statement (Annex **"Z"**) The transferee is entitled on completion to all unexhausted improvements[319] attached to the land at the date of contract, for they are part of it; and the disposition will transfer them with the land, without special mention.

4.3 Rights and Duties Between the two Dates

4.3.1 The contract (**Annex "H"**) would normally, and preferably should, define the rights and duties of the transferor and transferee between the two dates.[320] In the absence of a contract to the contrary,[321] the following propositions will apply:

(i) the transferee should pay or tender[322] the balance, if any, of the consideration **at the time and place of completion**;[323]

(ii) the transferee is entitled, **on completion**, to all unexhausted improvements which existed on the land at the date of contract (not date of completion);[324] and

(iii) **between the two dates**, the transferor must manage and deal with the property as carefully as a man of prudence would manage and deal with such property if it were his own.[325]

4.3.2 Land comprised in a contract for sale is in equity the property of the transferee as from the date of the contract. It follows that the transferor is not entitled to dispose of the Right of Occupancy to any other person, except subject to the contract; and such disposition will entitle the transferee forthwith to sue the transferor for damages if the transferor has incapacitated himself from performing the contract; or he may obtain an injunction restraining the transferor from carrying out such disposition to the plaintiff's prejudice. If, however, the transferor succeeds in alienating the property to another purchaser for money or money's worth, who takes free from the contract because it has not been protected by registration as an estate, the original transferee will have no other remedy than an action for damages against the transferor.[326]

4.3.3 In the absence of a provision in the contract to the contrary, either party may, **subject to the provisions governing dispositions**, voluntarily assign the benefit of his contract to another person. Thus if the transferor assigns the benefit of his contract to a sub-transferee, and notice of the assignment is given to the transferor, then, so long as the transferor is not thereby put to any extra expense, the sub-transferee is entitled to stand in the place of the original transferee, and can obtain specific performance against the transferor.[327]

4.3.4 On the death of the transferor, after the formation of a valid and enforceable contract, the purchase money forms part of his personal estate, and his rights under the contract can be enforced by his personal representatives, who have power to convey the land for all the estate and interest vested in the deceased at his death in any proper for giving effect to the contract.[328] On the death of the transferee, his equitable interest in the property vests in his personal representatives. If the transferee has specifically devised the property then, subject to provisions governing dispositions *inter vivos*, a proper assent in his favor and to any lien of the transferor for the purchase money, the devisee will take.[329]

4.3.5 Where there are encumbrances upon the property sold which are discharged out of the purchase money, the transferee should pay the proper amounts to the encumbrancers direct and only pay the balance to the transferor.[330]

4.4 The End Theme to Part One

4.4.1 The entire transaction should be closed down with a statement of account (**Annex "A1"**), especially so if one of the parties, or both parties, have retained experts [lawyer(s) or estate agent(s)] to carry out the transfer on their behalf.

4.4.2 In relation to transfer of Right of Occupancy, the **Land Act**, 1999 has modified current law in several respects. For example, provision covering virtually the entire transfer process is found under the Act itself. Approval of transfer shall be a prerequisite only where the Right of Occupancy was granted to the transferor less than three years before the transfer is to take effect, in other cases consent shall not be required but the transferor shall instead lodge a notification with the Commissioner for Lands. Such qualification does not exist under either the **Land Ordinance** or the **Land Regulations**, 1948; when it comes to approval, all transfers are treated alike.

4.4.3 With an eye on transparency, the **Land Act**, 1999 contains more elaborate provision concerning the formalities and procedure attending transfer. There shall be a presumption under the Act that an application for a grant of approval for a disposition shall be granted and that such application shall be determined by the Commissioner within sixty days or such other period as may be agreed upon by the Commissioner and the parties; and, if a determination is not made within the period aforesaid, approval to the disposition shall be deemed to have been refused. Under current law, there is no presumption of approval and the period within which an application shall be determined is not specified.

4.4.4 Moreover, under the **Land Act**, 1999, certain covenants shall be implied into instrument(s) relating to transfer of Right of Occupancy. The Act contains provision for the protection of creditors and third parties. It also contains provision for regaining possession by the transferor after concluding a contract for transfer of a Right of Occupancy; relief in favour of the transferee against rescission of such contract; and, relief in favour of the transferee against specific performance. Current law does not contain such provision.

4.4.5 As stated in paragraph 3.82 above, upon repeal of the **Land (Law of Property and Conveyancing) Ordinance**, the paternalistic approach to processing of transfer will be somewhat toned down. "Somewhat" because even the **Land Act**, 1999 contains restrictions against holding of land by non-natives: a non-citizen shall not be given land unless it is for investment purposes under the **Tanzania Investment Act**, 1997. More specifically, the repeal will do away with the License to Hold Land by Body Corporate now prescribed under that Ordinance for a foreign body corporate. But even under the **Land Act**, 1999, a transfer shall be subject to other relevant law.

4.4.6 Part Two is the actual manual for transfer of Right of Occupancy. It contains a checklist of steps that make up a transfer, a matrix showing the circulation of some essential documents and a number of annexes. The checklist sets out the procedure for transfer of Right of Occupancy, while the annexes carry relevant statutory provisions, specimen forms, scales of duties and fees payable.

4.4.7 Admittedly, the preceding discussion to a very large extent contemplates the ideal situation. That is to say, a transfer involving a Certificate of Occupancy as opposed to a mere Letter of Offer of Right of Occupancy. But, once accepted, such Letter is, *prima facie*, also evidence of a Right of Occupancy. A real practical problem sometimes faced by relevant officials is the difficulty in distinguishing authentic from forged Letters of Offer of Right of Occupancy. Registration of the instrument under section 30(1) of the **Land Act**, 1999 will, therefore, go a long way towards solving this problem.

4.4.8 Provision, under the **Land Act**, 1999,[331] concerning the validation of certain dispositions completed before that Act comes into operation merit a separate study that must be backed up by careful research on the ground. It may only be mentioned here that under said provision a person who acquires land under a disposition governed by customary law shall be deemed to be in lawful occupation thereof for six years, or other longer prescribed period, after the commencement of the Act and may, within that period, apply for and obtain a Certificate of Validation for not less than 33 years.[332] A person who fails to apply for such Certificate shall be deemed to be holding a license for six years, or other longer prescribed period, after the commencement of the Act. He may, however, apply for a Right of Occupancy in the regular fashion.[333]

4.4.9 Transparence in processing approval of transfer of Right of Occupancy can be further enhanced by predictability. Coming to mind is Land Form 15, titled "DISPOSITION OF LAND". The Form is, in essence, a checklist of the various elements of the disposition process.

4.4.10 The first part of the Form addresses details like the date the application for approval is received, tenure of property, nature and date of disposition. Also the parties and their races and whether Regulation 3 of the **Land Regulations**, 1948 applies to the disposition. This part would cover disposition of Right of Occupancy and other interests such as lease. Before April 1970, when they ceased to exist, this part also applied to Government Leases.

4.4.11 Part B of the Form applies only to Rights of Occupancy. It touches such matters as title number, term of the Right, payment of consent fees and land rent, whether the disposition will entail division of the Right. Other matters covered under Part B include whether the development covenant has been complied with, whether there is any evidence of breach of conditions and whether the disposition may result in breach of conditions.

4.4.12 Part C of the Form, which applied only to Government Leases, is now redundant. Part D of the Form applies only to dispositions requiring approval under section 11 of the **Land (Law of Property and Conveyancing) Ordinance**, which governs dealings in land between natives and non-natives. It looks at evidence of title, whether the Right is of a type that can be held by a non-native, whether there are burdensome conditions affecting the native and the Area Commissioner's (now District Commissioner's) recommendations.

4.4.13 Part E of the Form is employed to establish whether Stamp Duty has been paid, and the action to be taken in the event of non-payment. Part F of the Form is concerned with the fact of approval. Among the matters covered is whether the Commissioner has received a prohibitory order, caution, caveat or encumbrance. There is also space for land Officer's remarks, including any reason why disposition should not be approved. The Commissioner of Lands or a Land Officer, as the case may be, has three options. These are to approve the disposition, to refuse approval or to approve the disposition subject to annexure of development requirements.

4.4.14 The office of the Commissioner for Lands administered the Form. Regrettably, in more recent years the Form has largely fallen into disuse. Admittedly, a good number of its components may have become redundant. Nonetheless, it is strongly recommended that when making forms to be employed under the **Land Act**, 1999, the Form should be reintroduced with the necessary modifications, and its use in processing dispositions should be made mandatory.

---

[312] Section 2(1)(h) of the **Law of Contract Ordinance**.

[313] Section 2(1)(e) of the **Law of Contract Ordinance**.

[314] Date is the specification or mention, in a written instrument, of the time (day, month and year) when it was made (executed). The word is derived from the Latin word "datum" meaning given and is defined as the time given or specified- in some way ascertained and fixed. The time when an instrument was made, acknowledged, delivered or recorded; the clause or memorandum, which specifies that fact; and the time from which its operation is to be reckoned. That part of a deed or writing, which expresses the day of the month and year in which it was made or given. When we speak of the date of a deed, we do not mean the time when it was actually executed, but the time of its execution as given or stated in the deed itself. See **Black's Law Dictionary**, op. cit., p. 395.

[315] The precise meaning of date, however, depends upon context, since there are numerous instances when it means actual as distinguished from conventional time. See **Black's Law Dictionary**, op. cit., at page 395.

[316] **Encyclopaedia of Forms and Precedents**, Fourth Edition, Volume 18 (London: Butterworths, 1969) para. 551, p. 279. The vendor is so far a trustee for the purchaser that he is under a duty to preserve the property in the state in which it was when the purchaser agreed to buy it. The vendor is not, however, liable for accidental deterioration of the property, which does not occur through his own negligence.

[317] **Encyclopaedia of Forms and Precedents**, op. cit., para. 550, p. 279. Suffice it to say that the transferor would be well advised to obtain full payment before the transfer is registered, lest he loses the lien.

[318] Section 41(2) of the **Land Registration Ordinance**. Registration, under section 34 of the Ordinance, constitutes actual notice of the interest registered to all persons

and for all purposes connected with the land affected. In general this prevents any person claiming to be a purchaser without notice of the registered estate. As regards completion of dispositions of registered land, it stated in the **Encyclopaedia of Forms and Precedents**, op. cit., para. 651, p. 327 that, a transfer or other disposition of registered land must be completed by registration in order that a legal estate or interest will pass.

[319] Under section 2 of the **Land Ordinance**, means any thing or any quality permanently attached to the land, but does not include the results of ordinary cultivation other than standing crops and growing produce. It is the equivalent of a "fixture" under English law. Under section 2 of the **Land Act**, 1999, "unexhausted improvement" means any thing or any quality permanently attached to the land and includes trees, standing crops and growing produce whether of an agricultural or horticultural nature. In short, the new definition, apart from being more elaborate (includes protection of the environment), substantively reproduces the existing definition.

[320] See, for example, Atul Motilal Setalvad, **Mulla on the Transfer of Property Act, 1882** (Bombay: N. M. Tripathi Private Ltd., 1973) para. 55, p. 311.

[321] Sometimes the contract for the sale of property might merely specify the names of the parties, a description of the property, and a statement of the price. In Osborn, A **Concise Law Dictionary**, op. cit., p.229, such contract is called an open contract. See footnote 91, *supra*. At common law, the rights and duties of the parties under an open contract are: (1) duty of vendor (a) to show good title; (b) to abstract and produce documents; (c) to convey the identical property he has agreed to sell; (2) obligation of purchaser (a) to bear the cost of producing certain documents; (b) to examine the abstract at his own expense; (c) to complete the contract. In Tanzania this scheme of things is somewhat modified by land registration. Production of title and what has been said regarding abstract, for example, have been overtaken by the desirability to search the land register. Of course, parties may incorporate, wholesale, all of the aforesaid rights and duties. But that shall not absolve the transferee from the consequences of *caveat emptore* (let the buyer beware) should he neglect to inspect the land register.

[322] A transferor is, of course, not bound to accept anything but legal tender in payment of his purchase money. Thus he is not bound to accept a cheque. But payment in banker's draft is acceptable. See, in this connection, **Encyclopaedia of Forms and Precedents**, op. cit., para. 644, p. 324.

[323] **Mulla on the Transfer of Property Act, 1882**, op. cit., para. 55(5)(b), p. 313.

[324] Compare with para 55(1)(f) at page 312 in **Mulla on the Transfer of Property Act, 1882**, op. cit.

[325] Compare with para. 55(1)(e) at page 311in **Mulla on the Transfer of Property Act, 1882**, op. cit., and with footnote no. 187, *supra*. Moreover, the transferor must perform all the conditions, express or implied, subject to which he holds the Right of Occupancy up to the date fixed for completion; see **Encyclopaedia of Forms and Precedents**, op. cit., para. 55, p. 279.

[326] **Encyclopaedia of Forms and Precedents**, op. cit., para. 553, p. 280.

[327] **Encyclopaedia of Forms and Precedents**, op. cit., para. 554, p. 280. Compare with the case of *Juma Sultani Mkugenzi v. Ramadhani Amin Sultani* [1991] op. cit., in which Court granted specific performance against a successor in title.

[328] **Encyclopaedia of Forms and Precedents**, op. cit., para. 556, p. 281. Compare

with the case of *Juma Sultani Mkugenzi v. Ramadhani Amin Sultani* [1991] op. cit., in which a transferee was able to enforce against a successor in title, by way of specific performance, obligations traceable to a deceased transferor.

[329] **Encyclopaedia of Forms and Precedents**, op. cit., para. 557, p. 282.

[330] **Encyclopaedia of Forms and Precedents**, op. cit., para. 557, p. 282. If the encumbrance is a mortgage, the transferee must, upon paying off the encumbrancer, require the transferor to obtain, as the case may be, a discharge (**Annex "E"**) or a release (**Annex "F"**).

[331] Sections 53 to 55 of the **Land Act**, 1999. See parallel provisions in **A Draft Bill for the Land Act, Arrangement of Clauses**, which are clauses 117, 118 and 119. See also **Clause-by Clause Commentary, A Draft Bill for the Land Act**, op. cit., where it is stated that clauses 117 to 119 (sections 53 to 55 of the **Land Act**, 1999) "attempt to deal with the manifold problems of unauthorised market transactions which have been taking place for many years. The view is taken that these cannot be ignored or the fiction maintained that all the people who have 'paid' for land have no rights and are only squatters, liable to be dispossessed without compensation at any time. The clauses proceed on the basis that a market for land has existed for several years and must be recognised. The clauses are somewhat complex but this is because they are dealing with a complex situation."

[332] Section 53 of the **Land Act**, 1999.

[333] Section 54 of the **Land Act**, 1999.

PART TWO

MANUAL FOR THE TRANSFER OF RIGHTS OF OCCUPANCY

CHEKLIST FOR TRANSFER OF A RIGHT OF OCCUPANCY

Following client's instruction and deposit fees proceed to:-

Following client's instruction and deposit fees proceed to:

Stage	Task	Annex
1.	Conduct search, If acting for transferee, obtain transferor's responses to the questionnaire	C
2.	If search and the questionnaire disclose an Encumbrance, e.g., mortgage: a. Obtain redemption statement from Mortgagor b. Upon redemption, obtain discharge	B D I
3.	Conduct on-site inspection in order to form some opinion about state of repair and value of the property.	
4.	Establish current open market value of property.	G
5.	Draft sale agreement specifying date of completion. If a party resides outside Tanzania his signature must be notarised by a NOTARY PUBLIC;	H
6.	Draft deed of transfer adopting the format specified in the Land Registration Ordinance, First Schedule, Form L.R.5. If a party resides outside Tanzania his Signature must be notorized by a NOTARY PUBLIC or witnessed by an "authorised witness" as defined Under section 93(2) of the Land Registration Ordinance;	A
7.	Advise parties to execute engrossed sale agreementand deed of transfer simultaneously.	A, H
8.	If at the execution of deed of transfer and sale Agreement the transferee deposits a sum towards Purchase price: a. Draw a receipt for the deposit b. If deemed appropriate, lodge a caveat	 J K
9.	Obtain Certificate of Clearance of Land Rent in Respect of the property sold;	R
10.	Establish cost of construction of the property by Reference to actual cost or market cost;	P,Q
11.	Complete Capital Gains Tax Questionnaire;	M
12.	Submit Capital Gains Tax Questionnaire to Income Tax Department with the following annexes: a. Assessment of cost of construction b. Valuation Report, c. Sale Agreement as executed, so as to facilitate assessment of capital gains tax.	N
13.	Pay Capital Gains Tax and obtain Capital Gains Tax Clearance Certificate.	O
14.	a. Process consent to disposition pursuant to Regulation 3 of the Land Regulations, 1948 by submitting the deed of transfer as executed in	I

Stage	Task	Annex
	duplicate, the Certificate of Occupancy and one (1) copy each of Valuation Certificate of Report, Clearance of Land Rent Capital Gains Tax Clearance Certificate and Sale Agreement. b. Pay consent fee	L
15.	a. Seek registration of the relevant Right of Occupancy in the transferee's name by tendering to the Registrar of Titles the deed of transfer as approved in duplicate, the Certificate of Occupancy and one (1) copy of each of Certificate of Clearance of Land Rent and Capital Gains Tax Clearance Certificate. b. Pay registration fees.	S X
16.	Ensure that parties observe their obligations between date of execution and completion date.	
17.	Compile completion statement and ensure that transferor surrenders Certificate of Occupancy to transferee	Z
18.	Prepare and submit to client a Statement of Account showing fees due to advocate(s)	A1

CIRCULATION OF DOCUMENTS

Annexure	Subject Matter
C	Application for an Official Search 1. Applicant 2. Land Registry
G	Valuation Report 1. Transferor 2. Transferee 3. Income Tax Department 4. Commissioner for Lands 5. File Copy 6. Flimsy
H P,Q	**Sale Agreement as for Valuation Report, above** Assessment of Cost of Construction 1. Income Tax Department 2. Client 3. File Copy
S	Application for Registration 1. Land Registry 2. Client

CIRCULATION OF DOCUMENTS

Annexure	Subject Matter
C	Application for an Official Search 1. Applicant 2. Land Registry
G	Valuation Report 1. Transferor 2. Transferee 3. Income Tax Department 4. Commissioner for Lands 5. File copy 6. Flimsy
H	Sale Agreement as for Valuation Report, above
P,Q	Assessment of Cost of Construction 1. Income Tax Department 2. Client 3. File Copy
S	Application for Registration 1. Land Registry 2. Client

ANNEX "A"

The Land Registration Ordinance (Cap. 334)

TRANSFER OF A RIGHT OF OCCUPANCY

Title Number ....

In consideration of the sum of Shillings .... (Shs......................)
I .... of P.O Box ....
HEREBY TRANSFER to ...., a company incorporated in Tanzania and having its registered office ....
P.O. Box .... the Right of Occupancy registered under the above reference.
*

SIGNED and DELIVERED by the)
said .... who is known to me personally/identified)
to me by ....the latter being known to me personally)
in my presence this...............day of.............., ...)

Signature: ....
Postal Address: ....

A NOTARY PUBLIC

SEALED with the Common Seal of the)
said .... and **DELIVERED** in the presence of) SEAL
us this........................ day of....................,.....................)

Signature: ....
Postal Address: ....
Qualification: ....
Signature: ....
Postal Address: ....
Qualification: ....

* In the case of a transfer in consideration of natural love and affection, insert here the words "For purposes of Stamp Duty, the declared value is .... "

ANNEX "B"

SPECIMEN QUESTIONNAIRE TO VENDOR

1. Name and address of purchaser.
2. Name and address of purchaser's solicitors (if known).
3. Sale price.
4. Does the sale price include any chattels, e.g., carpets, curtains, gas or electricity heater, cookers, etc., which are separately valued?
5. In whose possession or custody are the title deeds? If the property is in mortgage, please state name and address of mortgagee and account no. (if any).
6. Is the sale dependent on the purchase of another property? If so, please give particulars.
7. Approximate completion date intended.
8. What boundary walls or fences have you maintained during your period of ownership? If no such maintenance has been carried out, which walls or fences do you believe to be yours?
9. Have there been any disputes as to rights of way, boundaries, etc.?
10. Do you share any facilities with adjoining owners such as right of way, joint drive-in, etc.?
11. Have any notices been served on you which affect the property?
12. Have any guarantees been given in respect of any repairs or treatment carried out to the property, e.g., woodworm, dry rot, etc.?
13. When was the building erected?
14. Is the planning permission (if any) in your possession.
15. Have any alterations or changes of use been made which need consent from the local authority or any other person or body?
16. Was the property purchased with the benefit of a mortgage. If so, give particulars of mortgage.
17. Is there a garage? If so, was it erected at the same time as the house?
18. Is there central cooling? If so, please confirm that it is free of any hire purchase or credit agreement.
19. Please confirm whether any of the following are included in the sale and will be left on the property: television aerial, electric points, wall or ceiling fittings, plants, shrubs, greenhouse, garden shed.
20. Are you removing any fixtures? If so, please specify.
21. Please give particulars of any Fire Insurance or Householder's

Comprehensive Policy.

22. Are you aware of being in breach of any covenant or condition affecting the property?
23. What is the ratable value of the property?
24. Is vacant possession of the whole property to be given? If not, please give particulars of any tenancy to which the sale is subject.
25. Please confirm that all the lessee's covenants in the lease have been duly observed and performed.
26. Has any demand or complaint been received from the lessor which has not been satisfied or complied with?
27. Please give particulars of all service or maintenance charges paid during the past three years.

Does your title include membership of any company or society having management of the property?

ANNEX "C"

TANGANYIKA LAND REGISTRY
APPLICATION FOR AN OFFICIAL SEARCH

To: The Registrar of Titles

Title No. ....

I, (We).....................................hereby request you to search the register in respect of the above title and advise me/us of the entries.

Fees: Shs. 4,000/= where C.T. Number is not supplied or Shs. 2,000/= where C.T. Number is supplied.

From: ....

P.O. Box ....

(Date) ....(Signature)

For Official Use

G.R.R. No............................ of ....issued

---

Search No.

OFFICIAL SEARCH

The following is a summary of the subsisting entries on

Property: District:

Title No..................

Place: ....

Description: ....

Area: ....

Tenure: **Right of Occupancy**

Term: Years from:

Rent: Shs .... Per annum (subject to revision)

Reservations: ....

Owner: ....

Incumbrances: ....

(Date)........................... Registrar of Titles ....

G P Dsm 4676/10-63/10m/2up

ANNEX "D"

Redemption Statement on A/C No:.................... Plot No:.................

TO: ....

Advance on 24.1.78	19,400.00
Add:Interest on advance	1,817.75
Add: Insurance premium	282.00
	2,099.75
Balance as at 31.12.78	21,499.75
Add:Interest 10% on balance	2,150.00
Add:Insurance premium	282.00
	2,432.00
Less:Repayments for 1979 806.60x4	
	3,226.40
	20,705.35
Add:Refund on repayments on 23.2.79	1,613.20
Add:Refund on repayments on 20.3.79	806.60
Balance as at 31.12.79	23,125.15
Add: Interest 10% on balance	2,312.50
Add: Insurance premium	282.00
Add: Advance on 17.10.80	26,800.00
Interest on advance	550.70
	29,945.20
	53,070.35
Less: Repayments for 1980 806.60 x 5 =	4, 033.00
	4,739.60
706.60 x 1 =	706.60
Balance as at 31.12.80	48,330.75
Refund on repayments onb/f	48,330.75
Refund on repayments onAdd: Interest 10% on balance	4,833.10
Add; Insurance premium	282.00
Add: Advance on 17.7.81	15,900.00

Add: Interest on advance	727.50	21,742.60
	70,073.35	
Less: Repayments for 1981 806.60x12	9,679.20	
Balance as at 31.12.81	60,394.15	
Add: Interest 10% on balance for 18 months Jan'82 – June 1983	9,059.10	
Add: Insurance premium for 18 months Jan'82 – June 1983	423.00	
Add: Advance on 14.7.85	17,900.00	
Add: Interest on advance	833.70	
	28,215.80	
Balance as at 31.12.82	88,609.95	
Less: Repayment for 18 months Jan'82 June 1983 M 092/P 32	2,419.80	
M 188/P 211	4,033.00	
M 092/P 32	5,646.20	
M 375/P 91	3,226.40	15,325.40
Balance as at 30.6.83	73,284.55	
Add: Interest 10% on balance Jan'82 – June 1983	7,328.45	
Insurance premium	282.00	
	7,610.45	
	80,895.00	
Less: Repayment for 1983/84 M 092/P 32	8,066.00	
Balance as at 30.6.84	**72,829.00**	
Add: Interest 10% on balance	7,282.90	
Add: Insurance premium	282.00	
	7,564.90	
Less: Repayment for 1984/85	**80,393.90**	

b/f	72,327.90	
Add: Interest 10% on balance for 3 months July-September 1985	1,808.20	
	74,716.30	
Less: Repayment from July-September 1985	2,419.80	
Balance as at 30.9.85	71,716.30	
Add: Interest 13% on balance for 6 months Oct'85-March 1986	4,661.55	
Add: Insurance premium	282.00	
	4,943.55	
	76,659.85	
Less: Repayment from Oct'85 – November 1985		1,613.20
Balance as at 31.3.86	75,046.65	
Add: legal & Ledger card fees	250.00	
Redemption figure Shs.	75,296.65	

PREPARED BY ....

CHECKED BY ....

APPROVED BY ....

ANNEX "E"

Form L.R. 15

The Land Registration Ordinance (Cap. 334)

DISCHARGE OF MORTGAGE

Title Number ....

We, TANZANIA HOUSING BANK a body corporate established by and under the provisions of Tanzania Housing Bank Act, 1972 of P.O. Box 1723, Dar es Salaam, Tanzania being the owner of the Mortgage registered as Filed Document Number ....**HEREBY DISCHARGE** the said Mortgage.

SEALED with the Common Seal of the said **TANZANIA**)
HOUSING BANK and DELIVERED in the presence of us) SEAL
this................day of 19 ....)

Signature: ....

Postal Address: ....

Qualification: ....

Signature: ....

Postal Address: ....

Qualification: ....

ANNEX "F"

Form L.R. 16

Title Number...............

The Land Registration Ordinance (Cap. 334)

RELEASE FROM A MORTGAGE OF PART OF THE MORTGAGE LAND

I,.......................................of..**HEREBY RELEASE** from the mortgage registered on Filed Document Number............ the land shown edged with red on the plan attached hereto.

(Signature and attestation).

ANNEX “G”

Valuation Report for Transfer of Property on Plot No.:................ Block .... Area...........

Date of Inspection 7th June, 1988

Owner:- The property belongs to .... of P.O. Box ....

Type of Building:- The property is partly a single storey and partly double storey commercial/residential property.

Situation:- The property is situated at the ....

Date of Construction:- According to information gathered, construction of the building started in ....and was eventually completed in ....

Tenure:- The Right of Occupancy in favour of the above person was issued on the .... for a term of .... Years at an annual rent of ....

Construction and Condition:-

This is a framed structure constructed of reinforced columns infilled with concrete blocks. The walls have been plastered and painted internally, and tyrolean rendered externally.

The Roof is of mono pitched type covered by corrugated iron sheets laid on treated timber purlins and rafters. There is a parapet wall all around the property.

The ceiling to the ground floor is of reinforced concrete slab and soft board whitewashed throughout, with the exception of the workshop and main garage where there is not ceiling.

Doors are pannelled in the garages and glazed in the showrooms and shops. The upper floor doors are of flush timber and are oil painted.

The windows are of glass casements with antiburglar bars and wiremesh in the garage and are of glass in the show rooms. Adjustable glass louvres in alluminium clips have been applied to the upper floor.

Cement screed floor finish has been applied to the garage and showrooms; thermosplastic tiles to the offices and bedrooms. Timber floor has been applied to the upper floor.

Access to the upper floor is by means of a timber staircase.

Accommodation comprises of:-

Ground Floor:-

- Managers office combined with secretary's office.
- Spacious shop with an adjoining Asian type wc, handwash basin has also been provided.
- There is a private office with good quality timber walling all around. It is also provided with a toilet western type with ceramic hand wash basin.
- Car hire department with good quality timber walling.
- Show windows are of glass panes.
- Accounts section with glass pane windows.
- Show room with glass pane windows.

Workshop:-

- There are different sections, which together form the workshop.
- There is a reception section
- The main workshop
- Oil and greasing section
- Panel beating section

Upper Floor:-

- The upper floor accommodates two flats.
- The first flat comprises one bedroom with built in wardrobes, a kitchen with a single drainer stainless steel wash hand basin, bath tub and low flush toilet.

The second flat comprises a spacious hall used as dinning and sitting room, six bedrooms two of them self contained with built in cupboards. Other bedrooms are fixed with built-in wardrobes. There is also a kitchen and store all with built-in shelves. There is a separate bath tub with toilet flush western type.

Outbuilding:-

There is one separate two storey building connected to the two sheds of similar construction to the main building. It has one store room, bonding room and two eastern high flush toilets.

Services:-
Electricity and water are provided from the public mains. Drainage is to the main sewer.

Siteworks:-
There is a cement screeded courtyard at the rear of the building. There is also a metal gate and boundary wall.

Planning:-
The property is zoned for commerical/residential use and change of use is not anticipated in the foreseeable future.

General Remarks:-
Wooden garages and workshop are all disused. Externally, especially on the western side, the building needs complete repainting.

Valuation:-
Its our opinion that the market value of the property is ....

General State of Maintenance:-
It is our considered opinion that the market value of the property in its existing condition is ....

VALUATION OF PROPERTY ON PLOT NO. ....

GROUND FLOOR:

a) Garage: 56.15m x 15.89m=892.2235
b) Showroom: 23.39m=371.6671
   Shop/offices: i) 16.23 x 15.89 – 257,8947
   22 x 11.20 x 11.20 x ° 197.127
   4.70m x 8.48m=455.0147=1718.90m² 39.8560

WORKSHOP:

a) 21.50m x 6.1=131.76m²
b) 21.60m x 6.58=143.34m²
c) Store/WC's 9.44 x 6.59 x 62.21m²=336.31m²

FIRST FLOOR

Injection room: 9.44m x 6.59 63.21m²

Flats:

main 17.83 x 21.50 = 372.60

22 x 10.60 x °= 176.57 546.16m²
Flat 1: 4.70 x 8.48=39.86 39.86m² 589.03m²

GROUND FLOOR

1718.90m² @7,000/= m²=	12,032,000/=

WORKSHOP

336.31m² @4,000/=m²=	1,345,000/=

FIRST FLOOR

Injection room: 62.2 @3,500/=m²	218,000/=
Flats2: 589.03 @8,000/=m²=	4,712,000/=
	18,307,000/=

COMPARABLES:

A Workshop and foundry at Njiro Hill was constructed at 1,000,000 in 1982. This gives a rate of 2,000/m²

Analysis for rating made in 1987 for factoris and godowns in Arusha showed a rate of between 8,000/= to 12,000/m²

Reinforced structure, including flats, offices, mainsonettes showed a rate of between 16,000 – 18,000/m².

These, however, are new buildings. Construction of the building being valued commenced in 1949 and was completed in 1962. Hence a rate of 8,000/m would be adequate for this structure. Market comparables are non existent as no transfers of this type of property have taken place.

ANNEX "H"

SALE AGREEMENT

THIS AGREEMENT is made the .... day of ...., 1988 **BETWEEN** .... of P.O. Box .... (hereinafter called "the Vendor") of the one party **AND** ...., a limited liability company incorporated in Tanzania and having its registered office at .... P.O. Box ...., Dar es Salaam (hereinafter called "the Purchaser") of the other part.

WHEREBY IT IS AGREED as follows:-

1. The Vendor will sell and the Purchaser will buy all that piece or parcel of land situate at Plot No. ....
Block .... And comprised in the Right of Occupancy registered under Certificate of Title No. .... Land Office No. .... together with all buildings and other improvements existing thereon at the purchase price of Shillings .... (T.Shs. ....) free from any encumbrance, lien or third party notice.

2. The purchase price shall forthwith be deposited with .... for the purchaser with instructions that the balance thereof be paid to the vendors upon the due registration of the Deed of Transfer and delivery of vacant possession of the property to the Purchaser.

3. The parties hereto agree that they shall simultaneously with the execution of this Agreement execute a Deed of Transfer for the conveyance of the property by the Vendor to the Purchaser and shall use their best endeavors to seek and obtain or cause to be sought and obtained consent from the Commissioner for Lands or other officer duly authorised in that behalf to this disposition.

4. This Agreement and the Deed of Transfer to be executed by the parties simultaneously herewith are subject to the consent of the Commissioner for Lands being accorded to this disposition. If such consent shall be refused, this Agreement shall become null and void and the Vendor shall forthwith refund any monies (including any fees or expenses) that shall have been disbursed hereunder.

5. Until the date of completion and delivery of vacant and peaceful possession of the property to the Purchaser, the Vendor shall pay all

rates, taxes, assessment and other outgoings whether parliamentary municipal or otherwise imposed or charged upon the said property.

6. The Vendor hereby covenants with the Purchaser to pay satisfy and discharge all outgoings and liabilities in respect of the property until vacant possession thereof shall have passed to the Purchaser and further undertakes to indemnify the Purchaser against all notices proceedings claims and demands arising out of and in connection with or incidental to the breach by the Vendor of the warranties undertakings and covenants herein contained

7. The purchaser reserves the right of making such requisitions and objections as may arise on the examination of documents pertaining to this Agreement or as may be revealed by the usual searches and inquiries.

8. The Purchaser shall bear and pay the cost of stamp duty consent fees registration fees, and other disbursements reasonably arising out of and/ or incidental to the preparation and completion of this Agreement and the Deed of Transfer that shall become payable by virtue of this transaction and includes without prejudice to the generality hereof the Advocates fees and expenses.

IN WITNESS WHEREOF the parties hereto have duly executed these presents in the manner and on the dates hereinafter appearing.

SIGNED and **DELIVERED** by the said ....)
who is known to me personally/identified to me)
by ....;)
the latter being known to me personally,)
in my presence this............ day of .... , 19........)

Signature: ....
Postal Address: ....

A NOTARY PUBLIC

SEALED with the Common Seal of the)
said .... and **DELIVERED** in the presence of) SEAL
us this....................... day of..................,....................)
Signature: ....
Postal Address: ....
Qualification: ....

ANNEX "I"

THE LAND ORDINANCE (CAP. 113)
REGULATIONS
Made under section 21
THE LAND (FEES) (AMENDMENT) REGULATIONS, 1974

1. These Regulations may be cited as the Land G.N. 1960 (Fees) (Amendment) Regulations, 1974 and shall be read No. 111as one with the Land (Fees) Regulations.

2. The Schedule to the Land (Fees) Regulations, is hereby amended as follows:-
   (a) by deleting item No. (7);
   (b) by deleting item No. (8A) and substituting therefor the following:-

   "(8A) Any approval by the Minister or any officer exercising any powers or duties under the Land ordinance which have been lawfully delegated to him by the Minister given under and in terms of Regulation 3 of the Land Regulations (as amended from time to time) in respect of a Right of Occupancy save in respect of any disposition held by a Native for a term which does not exceed 5 years or which is terminable by the Minister on or before the expiration of 5 years after the date of the disposition or in pursuance of a covenant contained or implied in a right of Occupancy:-

TShs.

(i)	where the consideration is less Shs. 2,000/=	50/=
(ii)	where the consideration is or exceeds Shs. 2,000/= but is less than Shs. 30,000	100/=
(iii)	where the consideration is or exceeds Shs. 30,000/=	2,000/=

BY COMMAND OF THE PRESIDENT

Ministry of Lands, Housing
And Urban Development,
Dar es Salaam.

B.A. SIKILO
24th February, 1974 Principal Secretary

ANNEX "J"

ACKNOWLEDGEMENT

I, ... hereby acknowledge to have received from .... The sum of shillings .... being part payment of the sale price of the property situate on Plot No. ....

Dated at Dar es Salaam this .... day of .... 19......

Witness to the above signature:

Signature: ....
Postal Address: ....
Qualification: ....

ANNEX "K"

The Land Registration Ordinance (Cap. 334)

Title No. ....

CAVEAT

(Section 78(1))

1. I,.. of ....
(hereinafter called "**the Caveator**") **CLAIM** an interest in the land registered under the above reference and REQUIRE a Caveat to be entered against the estate registered in the name of ....
2. I solemnly and sincerely declare that the land is subject of a Deed of Transfer of the Right of Occupancy in respect of the said land executed by the said .... and the Caveator and that the consideration of Shs. ..../= in respect of the transfer has been made.

AND

I make this solemn declaration conscientiously believing the same to be true and by virtue of the Statutory Declarations Act, 1966.

SIGNED and **DELIVERED** by the said................ who is)
known to me personally, in my presence this day of 1988)

Signature: ....
Postal Address: ....
Qualification: ....

ANNEX "L"

The Stamp Duty Act, 1972

SCHEDULE

STAMP DUTY ON INSTRUMENTS

Article No....................

Description of Instruments

Proper Stamp Duty

Article No.	Description of Instruments	Proper Stamp Duty Tshs
22	CONVEYANCE, not being a transfer charged or exempted under No. 60	Shs. 100/=
	(a) where the amount or value of consideration for such conveyance does not exceed Shs. 20,000/=	Shs. 40/=
	(b) where the amount exceeds Shs. 20,000/= for every Shs.1,000/= part thereof.	Shs. 40/=
	Provided that in any case where an agreement for sale is stamped with the *ad valorem* duty required for a conveyance, and a conveyance in pursuance of such agreement is subsequently executed, the duty on such conveyance shall be reduced by the amount of the duty paid on such agreement, but shall not be less than Shs. 100/=. Provided also that in the case of a decree or order, for or having the effect of an order foreclosure, the the *ad valorem* Stamp Duty upon any such decree or order shall not exceed the duty on a sum equal to the value of the property to which the decree or order relates, and where the decree or order states that value that statement shall be conclusive for the purpose of determining the amount of the duty and where *ad valorem* Stamp Duty is paid upon such decree or oder, any conveyance following upon such decree or order shall be dutiable with Shs. 4/=, under the provisions of section 6 of this Act: And provided also that the duty on a conveyance by the liquidator for of a company in liquidation of property forming part of the assets of the company to shareholder in the course of the dissolution of the company shall be Shs. 100/=	
	Exemptions Conveyance of any property under the Administrator – General's Ordinance to a Trustee, their or beneficiary if falling under Article 60(e).	
60	TRANSFER (whether with or without consideration)-	The same duty as company or other body
	(a) of shares in an incorporated corporate;	a Mortgage (No.39) corporate; for a consideration equal to the value of the shares.

Article No.	Description of Instruments	Proper Stamp Duty Tshs
	(b) of debentures whether debenture is liable to duty or not;	The same duty as a Mortgage or (No.39) for a consideration equal to the face value of the Debenture.
	(c) of any interest secured by a bond, mortgage-deed or policy insurance:- (1) if the duty on such bond, mortgage deed or policy does not exceed ten shillings;	The duty with which such bond, mortgage deed or policy is chargeable. Shs. 100/=
	(2) in any other case;	Nil
	(d) of any trust-property without consideration from one trustee or from a trustee to a beneficiary	Nil
	(e) of any property under the Administrator – General's Ordinance to a trustee, their or beneficiary.Provided that in any case where an agreement for sale is stamped with the *ad valorem* duty required for a transfer,and a transfer in pursuance of such agreement is subsequently executed, the duty on such transfer shall be reduced by the amount of duty paid on such agreement, but shall not be less than one shilling: Provided also that the duty on a transfer by the liquidator of a company in liquidation of property forming part of the assets of the company to a shareholder in the course of the dissolution of the company shall be ten shillings.	Nil
	Exemptions **Transfers by endorsement –** (1) of a bill of exchange, cheque or promissory note; (2) of a bill of lading, delivery order, warrant for goods, or other mercantile documents or title to goods; (3) of a policy of insurance.	
61	TRANSFER OF LEASE by way of assignment and not by way of under-lease.	The same duty as a for a considerat conveyance (No. 22) equal to the amount of the consideration for the transfer.
62	COUNTERPART OR DUPLICATE of any instrument chargeable with duty and in respect of which the proper duty has been paid:-	

Article No.	Description of Instruments	Proper Stamp Duty Tshs
	(a) if the duty with which the original instrument is chargeable does not exceed Shs. 100/=	Shs. 100/=
	(b) in any other case	Fifty per centum of the duty payable on the original, but not less than Shs. 100/= nor more than Shs. 200/=
	Exemptions (a) Counterpart or duplicate prepare and executed solely for the purposes of filing and record in the Land Registry,the Registry of documents or the Mining Registry. (b) Duplicate or copy of any contract of Service made under the provisions of the Employment Ordinance.	

ANNEX "M"

Income Tax Ref. No. ....

UNITED REPUBLIC OF TANZANIA
MINISTRY OF FINANCE - INCOME TAX DEPARTMENT
CAPITAL GAINS TAX PREMISES

In pursuance of the Provisions of Section 13 of the Income Tax Act, 1973, any person who sells in the United Republic of Tanzania any interest held by him in any premises or sells any premises owned by him is chargeable to tax on any gain realised from such transaction as laid down in the said Act.

Will you please let me have the following information regarding the premises sold by you and return the form together with the land Title(s) of the premises to the address given below.

Yours faithfully,

for: **PRINCIPAL ASSESSOR**

1. (a) NAME OF SELLER ....
   (b) ADDRESS OF SELLER ....
   (c) INCOME TAX REF. NO. ....
   (d) ACCOUNT NUMBER ....

2. (a) PREMISES ON PLOT NO. .... LOCATION ....
   (b) BLOCK NO. .... TITLE NO. ....
      (i) ORIGINAL COST OF CONSTRUCTION; SHS. ....
      (ii) PURCHASE PRICE IF OLD BUILDING: SHS. ....
      (attach Invoice and Receipts)

3. (a) PRESENT SALE PRICE: SHS. ....
   (b) NAME OF BUYER: ....
   (c) ADDRESS OF BUYER: ....
   (d) DATE OF SALE .... (Attach copy of Agreement

4. I, WE .... (name in full) Declare that the foregoing information is true and correct.

Date...................................... **Signature:** ....

N.B. Your attention is drawn to the provisions of Section 117 of the Income Tax Act, 1973 regarding offences and penalties for incorrect returns.

NOTES FOR THE PAYMENT OF CAPITAL GAINS TAX

All payments in respect of Capital Gains Tax Assessed by the Income Tax Department should be remitted to the Principal Collector of Income Tax, P. O. Box 806, Dar es Salaam in cash or Bankers cheque.

ANNEX "N"

THE UNITED REPUBLIC OF TANZANIA
MINISTRY OF FINANCE & PLANNING - INCOME TAX DEPT.
NOTICE OF ASSESSMENT - CAPITAL GAINS TAX

Ref. No. ....

Take notice that you have been assessed under the Income Tax Act, 1973. If you dispute this assessment you must give me notice in writing stating precisely the grounds of your objection within 30 days from the date of this notice of Assessment.

Signed: ....

Counter-signed:

PRINCIPAL
SENIOR ASSESSOR

Date: .... P. O. Box ....

NOTES SOURCE OF INCOME AMOUNT OF GAINS

Sales of Premise Plot No..
Principal Collect Payable on ....
P. O. Box 806 Payment slip: Ref. No. ....
DAR ES SALAAM

Name: ....
Address:...
Please accept payment of Shs. .... being Capital Gains
Tax on Premises on Plot No. .... Block ....
Official Receipt No. : .... Dates: ....
Delete whichever is not applicable.

ANNEX "O"

UNITED REPUBLIC OF TANZANIA
MINISTRY OF FINANCE
CAPITAL GAINS TAX CERTIFICATE

A. This is to certify that the assessed Capital Gains Tax amounting to Shs. .... (amount in words) .... consequent upon Sales of the premises (particulars of which are given below) has now been fully paid vide Income Tax Official receipt No. .... issued at .... on (Date) ....

OR

B. This is to certify that there is no Capital gains Tax in respect of Sales of premises particulars of which are furnished below:-

C. Premises on Plot No. ....Block No: ....
Title No.:..

Name of owner/seller of premises

Mr./Mrs/Miss/M/s ....
Post Address:..

Signature: ....

Valid only if endorsed by the Official Income Tax Seal (here)
....

Counter-signed: Principal Assessor/Senior Assessor
P. O. Box 9131

Date of Issue: ....

Delete whichever is not applicable.

ANNEX "P"
THREE (3) COPIES

Your Ref:
Our Ref:

TO WHOM IT MAY CONCERN

This is to certify that we have been Accountants and Auditors for................................ for about .... years.

The cost of construction of the property situated on .... Belonging to .... together with additions and improvements to the said property is shillings.....................................

This cost of construction has been obtained from a review of the old construction files, our knowledge of the client's financial status and from information obtained from the owner's personal recollections.

This, in our opinion, is a true and fair value of the original cost of construction with additions and improvements.

Yours faithfully

ANNEX "Q"

THREE (3) COPIES

Dear Sir,

VALUATION

We have consulted our records and find that some of the development carried out at .... Was designed by .... The areas of the various buildings are indicated on the attached plan.

We have split the types of construction in the same manner as shown on the drawing and added the area of the two storey sections. The main two storey concrete framed building is of very heavy construction and has high ceilings. The other buildings are of an industrial nature but solid construction. This development was built by .... So there are no records of the cost of construction nor of any contracts with building contractors. We have however taken building rates which agree with our records of the time and these are set out below:

DESCRIPTION	AREA sq ft.	Rate	Cost Shs
2 Storey RC Frame			
Flats & Offices	15,164	200	3,032,800
Heavy Workshops	13,162	110	1,447,820
Open Service Bays	3,540	85	300,900
Service Bay	576	85	48,875
Brake Bonding 2 fls.	1,276	160	204,160
Water storage tanks			33,717
		Shs.	5,034,555
And pumping equipment			500,000
		Shs.	**5,534,555**

We consider this a fair estimate of the cost of the development at the time. We trust this is sufficient for your purposes.

Yours faithfully

ANNEX "R"

THE UNITED REPUBLIC OF TANZANIA
MINISTRY OF FINANCE, ECONOMIC AFFAIRS AND PLANNING

Regional Customs & Sales Tax
P. O. Box 665
DAR ES SALAAM

Ref. No. IRD.29/6 .... Date ....

To: The Registrar of Titles
Ministry of Lands, Housing &
Urban Development
P. O. Box 9123
DAR ES SALAAM.

LAND RENT AND SERVICE CHARGES CLEARANCE CERTIFICATE MADE UNDER SECTION 41(I)(a) OF THE LAND REGISTRATION ORDINANCE OF CAP. 334

Plot No. .... Block No. .... L.O.N. ....
C.T. No. .... VRE No. .... Location ....
Ownership/Municipality/City. Owner/s ....

In exercise of the powers conferred upon the Commission for Land Rent and Service Charges Under Section 41(I)(a) of the Land Registration Ordinance, and his subsequent delegation of functions vide his appointment letter No. TY/L/40/5/VOL.E/578 of 18th December 1981, I hereby certify that the Land Rent Service Charges on the above mentioned land held under Right of Occupancy has been duly paid by the owner up to and including .... and that there are no liabilities outstanding.

1. Name: ....
   Signature:..
   Internal Revenue Officer ....
   District ....
2. Name: ....
   Signature: ....
   Regional Finance Officer ....
   Region .... Date ....

N.B. This certificate is only valid when signed by the Internal Revenue Officer and counter signed by the Regional Finance Officer.

c.c. The Commissioner for Land and Services Charges,
Ministry of Finance, Economic Affairs and Planning,
P. O. Box 9111
DAR ES SALAAM.

ANNEX "R"

To be lodged in duplicate Form L.R. 66

TANZANIA LAND REGISTRY

TO: THE REGISTRAR OF TITLES TITLE NO.......

The following documents are tendered for registration together:

1. Certificate of Title No. ....
2. ....
3. ....
4. ....
5. The following fees and stamp duty are tendered:-

Registration.. Shs.................................
Stamp Duty on original .... Shs.................................
Stamp Duty on duplicate .... Shs.................................
Stamp Duty on triplicate................................ Shs.................................

TOTAL===============

FROM: ....

Date: .... Signature: ....

RECEIVED the above document in number, on ....at ....
a.m Registrar of Titles

FOR OFFICE USE ONLY

1. G.R.R. NO. .... of ....
2. Registration Refused
3. Requisition delivered
4. Memorial entered
5. Passed for registration
6. Signed by Registrar

ANNEX "S"

Form L.R. 29

The Land Registration Ordinance (Cap. 334)

Title Number.............................

APPLICATION FOR COMBINATION
(Section 82)

I,... Of
..

HEREBY APPLY for the combination of the parcels registered under the above reference.

Dated this .... day of.......................................

Signature: ....

ANNEX "U"

Form L.R.30

The Land Registration Ordinance (Cap. 334)

Title Number.................

APPLICATION FOR DIVISION

(Section 83)

I,.. of ....
HEREBY APPLY for the division of the land registered under the above reference into separate parcels in accordance with the plan attached hereto.

Dated this...day of.......................................

Signature: ....

ANNEX "V"

Form L.R. 31

The Land Registration Ordinance (Cap. 334)

Title Number........

APPLICATION FOR REPARCELLATION

(Section 85)

We, the persons named in the first column of the schedule hereto, being desirous of changing the lay-out of the parcels registered under the above reference and described in the second column of the said schedule HEREBY APPLY for the cancellation of the folios of the land register relating to such parcels and the preparation of new folios in accordance with the plan attached hereto, so that the parcels described in the third column of the said schedule may vest in the persons whose names appear against them in the first column of that Schedule for the estates which those person enjoyed in, and with and subject to all rights and obligations now subsisting in respect of, the corresponding parcels described in the second column of the said schedule.

THE SCHEDULE

Name of Present Parcel Corresponding New Parcels ....

Owners Numbers...

(Signatures and attestation).

ANNEX "W"

ATTESTATION CLAUSES

(1) Signed and delivered by the said ....Who is known to me personally, in my presence this ....day of ....
(Signature) ....
(Postal Address) ....
(Qualification) ....

(2) Signed and delivered by the said ....identified to me by ....the latter being known to me personally, in my presence this .... day of ....
(Signature)...
(Postal Address) ....
(Qualification) ....

(3) Sealed with the common seal of the said ....
and delivered in the presence of us this ....day of ....
(Signature)...
(Postal Address) ....
(Qualification) ....

(4) Sealed with the common seal of the said ....
and delivered in the presence of us ....
(Signature)...
(Postal Address) ....
(Qualification) ....
and of me.. to whom the above signatories are known personally, this ....day of ....
(Signature)...
(Postal Address) ....
(Qualification) ....

ANNEX "X"

Under section 114

THE LAND REGISTRATION RULES, 1954

THIRD SCHEDULE FEES

Number Item	Matter	Fees Shs. Cts
1.	On application for first registration and section 10: for the First shillings 1,000/= or part thereof, of the value of the estate the subject of the application	20.00
	For every shillings 1,000/= or part thereof in excess of shillings 1,000/= up to shillings 100,000/=	7.50
	For every shillings 1,000/= or part thereof in excess of shillings 100,000/=	5.00
2.	On application for the leave of the Registrar Under the proviso to section 10(1) to apply, for first registration out of time	200.00
3.	On a notice of adoption under section 1	20.00
	For registration of a grant of public land or of certificate of occupancy:- For the first Shillings 2,000/= or part thereof of the value of the land or right of occupancy	10.00
	For every Shillings 1,000/= or part thereof in excess of Shillings 2,000/= up to Shillings 100,000/=	5.00
	For every Shillings 1,000/= or part thereof in excess of Shillings 100,000/= up to 400,000/=	2.50
4.	For the issue of a certificate of title under section 35,38 or 39	40.00
5.	On application for an entry or registration in Land Registry of any Mortgage:-Where the consideration or value secured does not exceed. Shs 5,000	40.00
	Where the consideration or value secured exceeds	

	Shs. 5,000/= but not Shs. 10,000/=	50.00
	Where the consideration or value secured exceeds Shs.10,000/= but not Shs. 15,000/=	60.00
	Where the consideration or value secured exceeds Shs.15,000/= but not Shs. 20,000/=	70.00
	Where the consideration or value secured exceeds 20,000/=	80.00
	On application for any entry or any other inscription, In the Land Register or for the cancellation of any Memorial not herein expressly provided for: Provided that no fee shall be Payable for the cancellation of Any memorial under section III (2)	40.00
6A.	On application for the registration of a transfer of an estate in land (other than a transfer of a trust property from a trustee to a trustee or from a trustee to beneficiary or a transfer incidental to the reconstruction of a company or the amalgation of two or more companies) or for the registration of a lease:- for the first shillings 2,000/= or part thereof of the consideration or value,	10.00
	For every shillings 1000/= or part thereof in excess of shillings 2000/= up to Shs. 100,000/=	5.00
	For every shillings 1000/= or part thereof in excess of shillings 100,000/=	2.50
6B.	Where any application chargeable under Item No. 6 or 6A relates to two or more parcels, there shall be payable in addition to the fee prescribed above, for the second and each subsequent parcel	10.00
7.	On an application for registration of a title by a fee at the adverse possession of registered land rate prescribed under Item I above.	
8.	On an application for combination of two or more parcels under section 82: for each parcel to be combined.	15.00

9.	On an application for the division of a parcel under section 83 or for a reparcellation under section 85: for each parcel resulting.	15.00
10.	On application for the filing of a power of attorney under section 96 or on giving notice or revocation.	40.00
11.	On application to inspect the land register and the filed documents:for each parcel, where the applicant furnishes the number of the block and parcel.	10.00
12.	On application for a list of parcels in which any person has an estate or interest.	40.00
13.	On application for an official search in respect of any estate in any parcel: where the applicant furnishes the numbers of the block and parcel	20.00
	Where the applicant does not furnish the numbers of the block and parcel.	40.00
14.	For uncertified copy of any folio of the land Register or of any filed documents or of any extract from an index Map or any filed plan:-per single page or part of a single page.	5.00
15.	For certifying any document or extract Therefrom or any extract from an Index map or any filed plan.	10.00
16.	For rectification of the land register: in respect of one parcel	40.00
	in respect of two or more parcels: for the first parcel.	30.00
	For each subsequent parcel	10.00
	Provided that no fee shall be payable where the rectification was necessitated by any error or omission of the registrar.	
17.	For the taking of a statutory declaration by the Registrar:for taking the declaration.	10.00
	For every exhibit thereto	3.00

18.	For recording any change of name or address for the first parcel	20.00
	For the second and each sub-sequent parcel	5.00
19.	For approving the form of any Documents. Such fee as the Registrar may decide but may not exceed Shs.100.	

ANNEX "Y"

Form L.R. 32

The Land Registration Ordinance (Cap. 334)

APPLICATION FOR FILING OF A POWER OF ATTORNEY

(Section 96)

We, ... of ....
and .... of ....
being respectively the donor and the donee of a power of attorney dated the .... day of..
HEREBY APPLY that such power of attorney be filed in accordance with the provisions of section 96 of the Land Registration Ordinance.

(Signatures and attestation)

ANNEX "Z"

COMPLETION STATEMENT

To purchaser's solicitors (if acting for purchaser)

We thank you for your letter of .... Enclosing engrossment for the (conveyance) (assignment (transfer).

We now enclose completion statement, calculated to .... on completion, will you kindly let us have your undertaking for the payment of ....

To vendor (if acting for vendor)

We are pleased to report that this sale has been duly completed and we (accordingly enclose) (have accordingly paid to your bank as requested) our cheque for .... being the net proceeds of the sale as detailed in the enclosed statement.

ANNEX "A1"

STATEMENT OF ACCOUNT

.... presents his compliments to and begs to state that his inclusive fee for professional services in connection with the transfer of property on.

Plot No. ....TShs..
to.. Less balance on deposit
TShs.. (see attached Statement).

STATEMENT OF ACCOUNT

Opening Balance (if any) ....
Add Receipt(s) vide cheque No........................ of ....

Sub-total
Less: (1) Disbursement ....
(2) Costs..

Sub-total ....

Balance (if any) ....

STATEMENT OF ACCOUNT

(Breakdown)
Re: ....

Plot No: ....
Deposit Shs................................

Less:-

(1) Disbursements
(a) Sundries for 3 persons Shs................................
(b) Commission on expedited registration Shs................................

(2) Costs

(a) Capital Gains Tax	Shs..................................
(b) Search fee	Shs..................................
(c) Survey fee	Shs..................................
(d) Stamp duty	Shs..................................
(e) Value Added Tax	Shs..................................
(f) Valuation fee	Shs..................................
(g) Consent fee	Shs..................................
(h) Registration fee	Shs..................................
(i) Land Rent	Shs..................................
Sub-Total	Shs..................................
Balance (if any)	Shs..................................

ABOUT THE AUTHOR

Zebron Steven Gondwe was educated at the then Ardhi Institute; the Faculty of Law at the University of Dar es Salaam; and, the Law School at the University of Wisconsin, Madision, where he read International Real Estate Investment. He was called to the bar of the Tanganyika Law Society in 1991 and to the bar of the Zanzibar Law Society in 1997. For the past 20 years he has been teaching in the Faculty of Law at the University of Dar es Salaam.

He has an active interest in national development issues and was the Research Coordinator for the Presidential Commission of Enquiry into Land Matters1991-1992 as well as a Consultant to the Presidential Commission of Enquiry into Taxes and Revenuesc1990. In addition to his manual on transfers of rights of occupancy, he has published many papers on land law, agricultural law, investment and gender.

www.ingramcontent.com/pod-product-compliance
Lightning Source LLC
LaVergne TN
LVHW022058200926
848481LV00003B/970

* 9 7 8 9 9 7 6 9 7 3 8 8 4 *